JUDAISM

and

JUNGIAN

PSYCHOLOGY

J. Marvin Spiegelman, Ph.D.

UNIVERSITY
PRESS OF
AMERICA

Lanham • New York • London

Copyright © 1993 by
University Press of America®, Inc.
4720 Boston Way
Lanham, Maryland 20706

3 Henrietta Street
London WC2E 8LU England

Library of Congress Cataloging-in-Publication Data
Spiegelman, J. Marvin.
Judaism and Jungian psychology / by J. Marvin Spiegelman.
p.   cm.
1. Judaism and psychology.   2. Jung, C. G. (Carl Gustav),
1875–1961.   3. Mysticism—Judaism.   I. Title.
BM538.P68S65   1992   296.3'875—dc20   92–31377 CIP

ISBN 0–8191–8895–6 (cloth : alk. paper)

 The paper used in this publication meets the minimum requirements of
American National Standard for Information Sciences—Permanence
of Paper for Printed Library Materials, ANSI Z39.48–1984.

ACKNOWLEDGMENTS

I wish to thank the *Journal of Psychology and Judaism* for permission to reprint the following articles:
Struggling With the Image of God, Vol. 10, #2, 1986, pp. 100-111.
A Jewish Psychotherapist Looks at the Religious Function of the Psyche, Vol. 14, #4, 1990, pp. 213-224.
Jewish Pyscho-Ecumenism, Vol. 15, #2, 1991, pp. 95-112.

I am also grateful to Falcon Press for permission to reprint the following:
Judaism and Jungian Psychology: A Personal Experience, in Spiegelman and Jacobson, *A Modern Jew in Search of a Soul*, Phoenix, 1986, pp. 245-260.
Julia, The Atheist-Communist and *The Medium, Sophie-Sarah*, Chapters three and ten in *The Tree: Tales in Psycho-Mythology*, Phoenix, 1982, pp. 97-150 and 381-440.

Princeton University Press has permitted me to quote extensively from Jung's *Answer to Job*. The Jewish Publication Society is the source for quotations from Rabbi Joseph Soloveitchik's *Halachic Man*.

TABLE OF CONTENTS

Introduction   vii

Part I: Harmony

Jewish Psycho-Ecumenism (Univ. of Judaism, 1989)   3
A Jewish Psychotherapist Looks At The Religious Function Of The Psyche
(Association Of Orthodox Jewish Scientists, UCLA, 1989)   21
Struggling With The Image Of God (Cedars-Sinai Conference On
Psychology And Judaism 1986)   33
Judaism And Jungian Psychology: A Personal Experience   45

Part II: Disharmony

The Jewish Understanding Of Evil In The Light Of Jung's Psychology
(1988)   61

Part III: Harmony And Disharmony Together

Julia, The Atheist-Communist   87
The Medium, Sophie-Sarah   121

INTRODUCTION

Everything around me seemed enchanted at this hour of the night. The nurse brought me some food she had warmed—or only then was I able to take any, and I ate with appetite. For a time it seemed to me that she was an old Jewish woman, much older than she actually was, and that she was preparing ritual kosher dishes for me. When I looked at her, she seemed to have a blue halo around her head. I myself was, so it seemed, in the Pardes Rimmonim, the garden of Pomegranates, and the wedding of Tifereth with Malchuth was taking place Or else I was Rabbi Simon ben Jochai, whose wedding in the afterlife was being celebrated. It was the mystic marriage as it appears in the Cabalistic tradition. I cannot tell you how wonderful it was. I could only think continually: Now this in the garden of pomegranates! Now this is the mystic marriage of Malchuth with Tifereth! I do not know exactly what part I played in it At bottom it was I myself: I was the marriage. And my beatitude was that of a blissful wedding.
C.G. Jung, *Memories, Dreams and Reflections p. 294*

The above experience of Jung, a highlight of his life, took place in his 70th year, after a life-threatening illness, along with other mystical experiences of a similar nature involving both the Greek *hieros gamos* and the Christian *mystical marriage*. These capped a life filled with the religious quest along with psychological discipline, unique in his century and pathblazer for many since then.

With regard to things Jewish, the Jung of 1944, when the above experience transported him, was a far different person than he was as the son of a Swiss country pastor, growing up in a traditional European environment, or the courageous psychiatrist who learned from and supported Freud—one of the few non-Jews to do so in the early days. And he was certainly more conscious than the Jung of the 1930 s, living in the time when the world did not truly realize the enormous threat to the Jewish people in that same European environment.

As those who are likely to read this book already know, there has been a significant amount of commentary about the Jung who was, on the one hand, thought to harbor anti-Semitic sentiments and, on the other hand, a friend and teacher of many Jews. His school of psychology has had a large number of Jewish followers throughout the world, including Israel. The

vii

accusations of anti-Semitism arise from some papers he wrote in the 1930's which are more politically unconscious of that same danger than they are anti-Jewish. They have had a negative impact because of his discussion of "racial psychology" issues at a time when this had a very destructive ring indeed. Despite Jung's attempts at healing this breach and the excellent discussions of the whole issue (e g. by Aniella Jaffé of Zurich and James Kirsch of Los Angeles, among others), the problem resurfaces. I have had occasion, myself, to answer this sort of criticism when it arose in such respectable journals as *The Psychiatric Times* and the *San Francisco Library Journal* of the C. G. Jung Institute. My "Letters to the Editor" have been well-received, but I am most satisfied with the sort of verbal response I gave some time ago to a person lecturing in the Los Angeles area who presented the various troublesome quotes of Jung without going into the context or significance.

At that meeting, I said that, from the speaker's words, I hardly recognized the Jung I had read for so many years nor the Jung that I had occasion to see and hear during my time in Zurich, 1956-1959. And it was certainly very far from the Jung to whom I had gone in 1959, when I had completed my analytic training, to receive an analytic "blessing," just as I had received from my ancient grandfather when I went off to sea during World War II. The blessing from my two "grandfathers," one Jewish and one not, both deeply religious, had been very important for me, as one might imagine.

I went on to say that most Europeans, including the Jung of the 1930's, were very likely to be prejudiced toward Jews by the very fact that they were brought up in a Christian culture. As we know, the Christian myth includes many negative references to Jews other than the founders (most of whom were Jewish) and includes the belief that its own "chosenness" has superseded that of the Jews. A two-millennia history of highly negative indoctrination about Jews is bound to remain in the psyche of westerners, despite modern scientific and rational emancipation. Think only of Voltaire and many like him, despising Christianity and Jews alike! Even Jews are subject to these prejudices if they are educated in the western systems or even live there. Perhaps only some, deeply steeped in Jewish religion and tradition, are spared this. One might even say that all of us in the Diaspora are so exposed and affected.

Psychologically and anthropologically, everyone is brought up in the myth of his culture, tribe and people. It is a collective idea that one's own group is special, "chosen," if you will, in contrast to others. Tribes in South America, for example, confine the word for "people" to themselves; their neighbors are not. We now know that our myths arise from deep inside us and have multiple layers of nation, place, family and person, in addition to the larger groupings of tribe, culture, etc. mentioned earlier. Indeed, our depths also include our animal cousins, as well as our condition of being composed of material elements, as well as psyche or soul. Our entire psychotherapeutic enterprise, after all, is the attempt to make conscious all those unconscious assumptions which rule us, thus allowing us a modicum of choice and dispelling our blindness. For us Jungians, the word "myth" does not mean an untruth, but a fundamental image, story or belief system which we hold, often unconsciously. We are immersed in it, like the air we breathe.

All of this is preparatory to the statement that the Jung of the above quotation is a differently conscious person than the younger version, just as we all are. It would be impossible for an anti-Semite to have the mystical experience quoted above. I remember very well my first analyst telling me how anti-Semitic he had become, subject to the Nazi furor, before he became conscious of it. And he was not only a religiously believing Jew, he had spent a brief time in a concentration camp! So, it is a good idea for us to become aware of our personal and collective myth, in order to better "choose" as well as being "chosen," and try to spare our neighbors the worst of our projections. We would desire the same from them, would we not?

This brings us to the present book, how it arose and what its specific "take" on Judaism and Jungian Psychology might be. For some years, I have been co-authoring and editing a series of books on the general theme of the various religions and their connection with Jungian psychology. The first of these, *Buddhism and Jungian Psychology,* I co-authored with Mokusen Miyuki. The second of that series was less that of religion and psychology, but one of the general Jewish psyche at this time and its relation to Jungian psychology. It was called *A Modern Jew in Search of a Soul* and had some twenty-odd contributors, which I edited along with Abraham Jacobson. This was followed by *Hinduism and Jungian Psychology* (co-authored with Arwind Vasavada), *Catholicism and Jungian Psychology* (twenty-odd contributors), *Sufism, Islam and Jungian Psychology* (co-authored with Pir Vilayat Khan and some half-dozen others), and *Protestantism and Jungian Psychology* (twenty-odd contributors). I had planned to present a book at this point on *Judaism and Jungian Psychology* when my regular publisher announced that he was no longer going to continue the series, despite the fact of having sold out every one of them. Our relationship continues (he wanted to bring out my therapy books, for example), but he just decided not to go on with that topic for personal reasons.

That surprise "rejection" happened about the same time that another of its kind occurred. Several years ago, when I was invited to give a lecture at a workshop on psychology and Judaism, I chose to speak on the following topic: *The Jewish Understanding of Evil in the Light of Jung's Psychology.*

The paper generated a lot of intense discussion and interest. The editor of a well-respected journal thought that the article would be best served by having it as part of a special issue, with a number of discussants arranged for this and it was almost in press when the editor contacted me guiltily, saying that he was advised not to print the issue since it was too controversial. What was it that was of concern? The use of the word "Jesus" is most difficult for some Jewish audiences, I was told. I was surprised but not too much so, since I had included a specific part on this touchy problem in the paper itself.

So, here I was: eager to produce my specifically "Jewish" book in the series on religion and my specific attempt to bring the insights of Jung's *Answer* to *Job* to our Jewish understanding. My special "children" in this area were rejected; they were "orphans," even "abandoned." I realized that our theme itself has an implied pair of opposites in it, subject to both a harmonious and disharmonious relation. Rather than let these rejected ones suffer a fate of some *mamzerim*, however, I chose to continue honoring their parenthood in Judaism and Psychology and seek another publisher. The result is now in your hands. I have accepted the theme of Harmony and Disharmony and included it in the book. Part I of this book comprises some papers of mine in the general field relating Jungian psychology and Judaism, all of which were received without trouble. Part II comprises the controversial paper I wrote on "Evil" (is it surprising that "evil" should also adhere to it?) Part III expresses a union between harmony and disharmony: I have included stories I wrote as part of my fictional work, *The Tree,* in which people tell their own tales of individuation, each of which connects with a particular religious or spiritual orientation. A story from each of these has been included in all my books on Jungian psychology and religion; I continue the practice here, since the book is now out of print. These two tales are Jewish in nature; the first is of Julia, an atheist-communist who finds her way to her unique religious attitude, while the second, that of the Medium, Sophie-Sarah, is more mystical in nature and takes up the issue of the Holocaust. Their inclusion here is particularly relevant since they combine harmony and disharmony, individual and collective, positive and negative.

I trust that the reader will be stimulated by this presentation and, one hopes, aided in bringing further consciousness to himself/herself as well. In the event that anyone is offended by the material, I beg pardon in advance and welcome response. In these days, Jews are once again required to struggle to maintain their identity in a world which no longer automatically supports this as it did in the years immediately after the horrors of the Holocaust were known. I am reminded of what a Jewish Jungian colleague said about himself, something to which I resonate very much. He said that when he is with Jungians, he feels himself very much the "Jew" and a carrier of that particular kind of consciousness; when with Jews, he feels himself a carrier of the specifically Jungian viewpoint. In that regard, he is most at home in being "homeless." This "homeless" feeling, I do not share. Nowadays, thank God, we no longer have to identify with that specifically Christian image of the "Wandering Jew," but can connect ourselves to both Israel and the Jewish people, as well as our American nationality, while maintaining our individuality. If we can manage to remain "individual," yet linked with our nation and tribe, if we can both rise and sink to the heights and depths connecting us with all humanity and all life, then perhaps we will have honored what both Jungian Psychology and Judaism have offered to us. It is in the service of that spirit of Self and collective that my series of books on religion and psychology is brought into the world.

PART I: HARMONY

JEWISH PSYCHO-ECUMENISM

(A paper for the University of Judaism, Los Angeles, Fall, 1989)

The Holy One, praised be God, patterns every person after Adam and every one is unique. Therefore every person is obliged to say: For my sake was the world created.

Mishnah Sanhedrin 4:5

Deep in the heart of every Jew, in its purest and holiest recesses, there blazes the fire of Israel.

Rabbi Isaac Kook

We live at a time of unusual tension among the Jewish people. On the one hand, it has survived its worst historical tragedy in the Shoah and has found a miraculously vibrant home in Israel. On the other hand (as Tevye might say), it is suffering a tremendous conflict of opposing viewpoints. Disparity in attitudes toward religion, national destiny, and cultural patterns, as well as normal political and economic differences, lead to vituperation and vilification, so that even the unthinkable occurs: some Jews desecrate synagogues with Nazi swastikas; other Jews can support the dismantling of the state of Israel.

There has always been dynamic conflict among the Jews, e.g. Pharisees versus Hellenists, Mitnagdim versus Hassidim, but always in the context of one people attempting to serve the will of God. Since the Enlightenment, however, the conflict has deepened and intensified, so that now we see that the forces of assimilation and disintegration, especially in the Diaspora, are almost as great as those toward cohesion. It is a law of Jewish history that centrifugal forces tear away individuals and groups, while centripetal forces keep the body of the people together (Patai, p. 61), but it is apparent to all that this time of the ending of the current two-thousand year eon threatens a continuing apocalypse, even after the survival from the Holocaust.

A serious student of the Jewish mind, after a detailed examination of history and culture, concludes that Jewish survival in all times and places is based on two beliefs and two attitudes: belief in one God and His special relationship with the Jewish people; duty toward God and toward one's fellow human beings. Hellenized Jews remained monotheists, Goodenough tells us (Patai, 1977, pp. 64 ff.) even when they "admitted that divine reality

3

was expressed and manifested through Greek gods." Their style was Greek but their content was Jewish. And even in the days of Sephardic grandeur, the Jews wrote prose in Arabic, but poetry in Hebrew (Patai, 1977, p.103)! Regarding the other half of this capacity for survival, the question of duties, this same student concluded that Jewish values of family, education and charity have transcended all the variations and peregrinations among this people (Patai, 1977, p.482).

The present paper will examine some of the present-day diversity from what might be called a phenomenological, psychological and ecumenical point of view. This means, simply, that one approaches the varying viewpoints from "inside" rather than "outside"—that is to say, sympathetically and with an attempt at understanding before passing judgment—and with the aim of honoring each in the attempt at arriving at some transcending possibility of union. We shall also make use of the psychological discovery that the psyche itself is made up of opposites, and that consciousness is built up as a result of this process. This will become clearer later on.

We can begin with what one might call a triangle of conflicting parties within religious observance itself—leaving until later the issues of the non-observant—namely the Orthodox, Reform and Conservative. One begins, of course, with the Orthodox, since there was no other, really, in the long history of the Jewish people, until the Emancipation and Enlightenment at the time of Napoleon, two hundred years ago. For our grasp of the Orthodox viewpoint, we can probably do no better than appreciate the work of the outstanding scholar, Rabbi Joseph B. Soloveitchik, originally of the Lithuanian Mitnagdim, but also possessor of a fine secular German education and a long-time resident and religious leader in the United States. His book, *Halaskhic Man* (Soloveitchik, 1983), is a marvel of informed clarity, spiritual discernment, and religious appreciation; I would rate this book among the best in Jewish religious thought in this century.

We all understand that the covenant, Torah, and the Law are central for Orthodox Jewry, of course, but many of us might believe that they are single-minded, undivided, sure of their path and what they are. Not so, says Rabbi Soloveitchik. He begins his book with the observation that the man who is observant of *Halakha* lives a conflict of opposites (Solovetchik, 1983 p.3):

> *Halakhic* man reflects two opposing selves: two disparate images are embodied within his soul and spirit. On the one hand he is as far removed from *Homo Religiosus* as east is from west and is identical, in many respects, to prosaic, cognitive man; on the other hand he is a man of God, possessor of an ontological approach that is devoted to God and of a world view saturated with the radiance of the Divine Presence.

Halakhic man suffers, says Soloveitchik, from dualism, a deep spiritual split, "but he mends the split" through the concept of *Halakhah* and law: (p.69). Following this observation, Soloveitchik provides a long footnote which takes to task the simplistic religious belief, found in some Protestant groups and in American Reform and Conservative Judaism, that the religious experience is of a simple nature, tranquil and ordered, "an enchanted stream for embittered souls and still waters for troubled spirits." No, it is not this, he says, it is stormy with opposites. Furthermore, he is against "romanticism" and mysticism:

> The individual who frees himself from the rational principle and who casts off the yoke of objective thought will in the end turn destructive and lay waste the entire created order. Therefore it is preferable that religion should ally itself with the forces of clear, logical cognition, as uniquely exemplified in the scientific method, even though at times the two might clash... (p.141).

Halakhic man is like a mathematician, he says (p.19):

> When *Halakhic* man approaches reality, he comes with his Torah, given him from Sinai, in hand. He orients himself to the world by means of fixed statutes and firm principles... His approach begins with an ideal creation and concludes with a real one. (He is like) a mathematician who fashions an ideal world and then uses it for the purpose of establishing a relationship between it and the real world...

Such an observant Jew, furthermore, is interested in everything—sociological, commercial, marriage, all life (p.22)—but not at all in the transcendent world: "Better one hour of Torah in this world than the whole of the world to come" is how it is stated in the "tanna" (Avot 4:17). Why is this so? Because the *Homo Religiosus* proclaims that the "lower yearns for the higher," whereas *Halakhic* man declares, "the higher pines for the lower" (p.30). We are reminded of the Jewish Tree of life which has its roots in heaven and grows toward the earth, but that image is to be found in Jewish mysticism, suspect according to our Mitnagid scholar.

The thrust of *Halakhah*, furthermore, is democratic from beginning to end; no person needs the aid of others in order to approach God. No elitism here, but also no mystical direction either, opines our Rabbi. He is against *tzaddik* cults. Yet if we ask how it is that God enters the world, he tells us, just like the Kabbalists, that this occurs through *tzimtzum,* "contraction." Even "one square cubit" reveals "the awesome mystery that God contracts his divine presence in this world." We shall see this unexpected overlap with the mystical later on, but now, to our chagrin, we must reveal the antipsychological attitude of Rabbi Soloveitchik, consonant with his focus on "the empirical earthly life, the life of the body" (p.43):

> One must not waste time on spiritual self-appraisal, on probing introspections, and on picking away at the 'sense' of sin. Such psychic analysis bring man neither to fear nor to love of God, nor most fundamental of all, to the knowledge and cognitions of the Torah (pp. 74-5).

He values the psychological path no more than the mystical one, I regret to say, but that may be because he is not familiar with certain viewpoints and findings in that field, for example Jung's. In other places, his words sound familiar to one who is knowledgeable about the individuation process.

> Man, in one respect, is a mere random example of the biological species—species man—an image of the universal, a shadow of true existence. In another respect, he is a man of God, possessor of an individual existence (p.125).

Collective and individual are typical mutually necessary opposites for Jung, too. But when Soloveitchik talks about the movement from the self-awareness of repentance to becoming an independent personality, finally becoming a prophetic individual in relation to God and society, he could almost be describing the individuation path of awareness—knowledge of the Self as a transcendent aspect of one's own and collective Being, accompanied by creative renewal. "This is the path that the *Halakhah* has charted for man to travel," he tells us, and here he joins with the most advanced religious consciousness of our day.

I would like to conclude this thumbnail survey of Rabbi Soloveitchik's Halakhic Man with his most moving and modest conclusion, wherein, like another famous theologian, the Dutch Protestant Gerhard van der Leeuw, (van der Leeuw, 1938) the profoundly erudite scholar bows his head to God. He apologizes that his words are merely "fragmentary" on this topic and continues (p. 137):

> But it is revealed and known before Him who created the world, that my sole intention was to defend the honor of the *Halakha* and *Halakhic* men, for both it and they have oftentimes been attacked by those who have not penetrated into the essence of *Halakha* and have failed to understand the *Halakhic* personality. And if I have erred, may God, in His goodness, forgive me.

We turn, now, to the viewpoint in opposition to our hallowed one of orthodox adherence to *Halakha*, that which has become known as Reform

Judaism. Although a critical view of traditional Judaism was contained in a book written in 1638, probably by Leon da Modena, it was only in the middle of the 18th century that the forces of the Enlightenment, along with the general emancipation of the Jews, resulted in a movement for change which has not since subsided. The earlier struggle between the Pharisees and Hellenists, between the forces of cohesion and those aiming at integration with the gentile world, resulted in a victory for the former and was not seriously challenged for a millennium and three-quarters. But now, in the face of the Emancipation and other events which ultimately resulted in Napoleon's assembly of the Sanhedrin, the Jewish community simply had to accommodate to the modern world. Many people embraced the view that religion had no rights over its followers and must not resort to compulsory measures.

Among these people was Moses Mendelssohn (1729-1786), often called the father of the German Jewish movement of Enlightenment. Knowledgeable in traditional Jewish learning, he was also brilliant in German, French, Latin, philosophy, poetry and mathematics. As an able defender of Jewish rights, he went on to write a book called *Jerusalem, or on Ecclesiastical Authority and Judaism*, in which he gave the final expression of his view that it was of central importance to adapt to the mores of the country in which the Jews found themselves, but also to "cling steadfastly to the religion of the fathers." Despite his Herculean efforts to maintain this dual position, he was unfortunately unable to bridge the gap between Jewish values and modern culture. The result was that there was much subsequent assimilation and conversion among the Jews of his time, including four of his own six children.

This, of course, was the dire prediction made by the Orthodox, both then and now, who objected to the Haskalah (Enlightenment) on four grounds (Patai, 1977, p.255): (1) the acquisition of secular knowledge for its own sake, having nothing to do with Jewish life, would result in anti-Jewish ideas; (2) making *Halakha* non-obligatory would undermine observance; (3) changes in *minhag* (customs), such as wearing the caftan and the speaking of Yiddish, were sacrilegious; (4) participation in the life of the gentiles was a mistake, since Jews were enjoined to keep apart: "And ye shall not walk in their statues" (Lev. 18:3). These objections have turned out to be well-founded, alas, although, as we shall see, Reform has hardly died out and has continued now for over two hundred years.

If we ask ourselves, however, why Moses Mendelssohn's great vision of dual commitment failed for his own time, and possibly in the future, I think we have to look at an interesting event which took place when a friend of his, the Marquis D'Argens (1704-1771), chamberlain of Frederick the Great of Prussia, asked for privileges of "protected Jew" for Mendelssohn. In his letter to Frederick the Great (Patai, 1977, p.237), the Marquis said:

A *philosophe* who is a bad Catholic begs a *philosophe* who is a bad Protestant to grant the privilege to a *philosophe* who is a bad Jew. There is too much philosophy in all this for justice not to be on the side of the request.

This clever and sophisticated self-disparagement reveals that what all three "enlightened" men really shared was a belief in "philosophy" that transcended their natal faith. This is the hallmark of the modern age. Until the Age of the Enlightenment, religion was the main thing in everyone's life and the Jews remained an out-group. With Emancipation, their status was challenged. Formerly, the Jews were persecuted but united; now they were emancipated and enlightened, which led to the same disintegration of faith that occurred with the population of their host countries. As Patai has well expressed it (Patai, 1977 summary, pp. 271-274), the Jews achieved a triumph by entering into the enlightenment and providing the world with great thinkers and Nobel prize-winners. But they have also suffered a tragedy through the loss of their peace of mind and their connection with God.

But must it be so? Is it true that reform and adaptation must lead to assimilation and conversion? Kaufmann Kohler (1843-1926), leader in the American Reform movement, felt that religion had to do with moral progress and the chosenness of the Jews included the mission to effect it. Revelation, indeed, can only continue by reformation and purification. He says (Hertzberg, 1961, p.37):

> The election of Israel cannot be regarded as a single divine act, concluded at one moment of revelation, or even during the Biblical period. It must instead be considered a divine call persisting through all ages and encompassing all lands...

On another occasion, Rabbi Kohler put it even more passionately:

> The leaders of Reform, imbued with the prophetic spirit, felt it to be their imperative duty to search out the fundamental ideas of the priestly law of holiness and, accordingly, they learned how to separate the kernel from the shell... Only the fundamental idea, that Israel as a first-born among the nations has been elected as a priest-people, must remain our imperishable truth, a truth to which the centuries of history bear witness by showing that it has given its life-blood as a ransom for humanity... Not until the end of time, when all of God's children will have entered the kingdom of God, may Israel, the high-priest among nations, renounce this priesthood.

Such a commitment is truly a religious one, and this passion in Reform is not limited to an early period or person, The Reform movement continues apace in the United States and is even beginning to find some place in Israel, despite great opposition. From our psychological pint of view, however, we see this conflict as mirroring the opposition between the powerful forces toward cohesion versus those toward expansion, particularly in relation to the larger world. One can readily see the advantages and disadvantages of each of them, but before we do so, we must look at the third part of our triangle, the movement which aims at a reconciliation between these two opposites, namely the Conservative or Masorati movement.

The Conservative Movement began when its founder, Zechariah Frankel (1801-1875), dramatically left the Reform Rabbinical Conference held in Frankfurt-on-Main in 1845, horrified at what he saw as unwarranted attacks on Halakha, Jewish law. His first aim was to protect, but his second aim, (Siegel, 1977, p. xiii) was "to make change possible." This change should be gradual and in accordance with what Solomon Shecter later called, "Catholic Israel," by which he meant, "the body of men and women within the Jewish people who accept the authority of Jewish law and are concerned with Jewish observance as a genuine idea." This observance could be rigorous or not, but what was required was that people be sensitive to their non-observance and respect the authority of the law.

> When the Jewish community speaks authentically out of its own integrity, it is the medium through which the divine intention for the people is expressed... It is the collective conscience which gives the ultimate judgment about how the law should be changed and modified. (Seymour Siegel, 1977, p. xviii)

In other words, Jewish Law is seen as the "specifically Jewish expression of religiousness" (Ginzberg, in Siegel, 1977, p.1), the means by which the Jewish consciousness expresses itself. Change is possible when any particular law ceases to express this religious and ethical thrust. However, this change must be in accord with the spirit of the whole people.

When Frankel said, "Judaism is the religion of Jews," he meant such things as the maintenance of Hebrew as the liturgical language because it expressed that spirit and not just national convenience. In a similar vein, the sanctity of the Sabbath reposes not in the fact that it was proclaimed on Sinai, but in the fact that the Sabbath idea found for thousands of years its expression in Jewish soul. Thus the "Law" is essential in Judaism, not the laws.

How then, is change to come about? Several principles are recognized: (1) A non-fundamentalist view of revelation. We receive the same Torah as our fathers, yet "we who receive it are different and we hear it a different way" (Will Herberg, Siegel, 1977, p.153). Or as Franz Rosenzweig saw it, there is a distinction between Torah-as-written (Orthodox) and Torah-as-read (Conservative). (2) Discernment of the needs of the time; (3) Recognition of historical development; (4) Need for perspective; (5) Demands of *aggadic* and ethical aspects of Judaism; (6) The acceptance of pluralism in the religious community.

This latter point is a crucial one. It has resulted in the acceptance of *aliyot* for women in some places and not in others, for example. The first Conservative Israeli woman rabbi has been accepted in the United States, for example, but would not yet be permitted in Israel. Such a rule is based on local choice, or *kevod hatzibur*—that which offends one congregation may not disturb another. Such acceptance does not necessarily lead to wishy-washiness, however, because the Conservatives are eager to truly carry this dilemma. They wish to "renew and retain, to conserve and to progress." And, as Seymour Siegel has put it, They are devout in this aim: "We ask divine help in fulfilling this task."

Lest you are not convinced by this prayer, hear how a modern Masorati Rabbi, the revered Abraham Joshua Heschel expressed it (Siegel, 1977, p. 133):

> We must consider Torah as a vision of man from the point of view of God. If we consider God from the point of view of man, we can not even pray. Our problem is not how much halacha to observe, but how to pronounce it. We have almost forgotten how to spell it. We may totally forget how to recognize it.

Heschel told us, in a way one would not ordinarily expect from a Conservative adherent, that we should consider the *mitzvoth* not in terms of the rational meaning, but "compatible with the sense of the ineffable." This, in turn, will lead us to a well of meaning. Sounds quite orthodox, doesn't it?

> Judaism does not stand on ceremonies... Jewish piety is an answer to God, expressed in the language of *mitzvoth* rather than in the language of ceremonies. Ceremonies are relevant to men; mitzvoth are relevant (ways) to God. (Siegel, 1977, p.150)

In carrying out a *mitzvah*, we acknowledge the fact of "God being concerned with our fulfillment of His will." In so speaking, Heschel is not alone in this passion. Will Herberg, for example, (Siegel, 1977, p. 153), in 1953 wrote that "To be an authentic Jew is to affirm the true redemptive history, as opposed to the false or idolatrous redemptive histories of totalistic nationalism, communism or fascism. The authentic life of the Jew is truly existential," he says, and involves the entire being, thinking, feeling and doing. No commandment is automatic without regard to the circumstances.

I have now presented the three legs of our Jewish triangle, each impressive and valid. To summarize, let us see how the three differ on the

Covenant, the law. For Orthodoxy, the law is supernaturally revealed and unalterable, except through subsequent revelation or through reasoned interpretation consonant with tradition. Reform sees the law as a product of historical evolution and no longer functional in many ways; what survives fully are the ethics which are as binding as ever. Conservatism states that the law is binding because it is the expression of the religious spirit of the Jewish people; changes may be made but must not be arbitrary, in time or place, but only when universally acceptable.

Each view reveals a truth and each has a defect or shadow-side, as a Jungian would put it. For Orthodoxy, rigidity and excessive fundamentalism is the danger. For Reform, dissolution and assimilation is the feared result. And for Conservatism, there is not only wishy-washiness, but what an extremist in their own midst, Mordecai Kaplan, has expressed (Siegel, 1977, p.13): "Conservatives are afraid of doing a thing for the first time; a compromise between wishing to stand still and afraid to go forward." But the virtues of the three attitudes and equally visible: faithfulness versus freedom versus fairness.

The conflict among our viewpoints centers on the Covenant and how to live it. If we look at the Covenant itself, however, we can see that conflict is already contained in it, as potential. As Herzberg pointed out (1961, p. 11), the Covenant is of two types, particular and universal; the former is that of a people that God chose to His priesthood; the latter is that God exists in the world and cares for all people. Even the Covenant itself is simultaneously for all People (through Noah and the Noahide laws) and the Jews particularly. Whether one focuses on the former or the latter is at issue, since all viewpoints accept both charges but emphasize different parts of them.

To look at it from the point of view of Patai's two beliefs and two duties, mentioned earlier: Do we focus on our duty to God or to our fellow man and all humankind: And how do we reconcile these? It is apparent to me that the bearing and acceptance of conflict is implied in all three viewpoints, a psychological condition which is much appreciated in contemporary psychological understanding as the ground for spiritual growth.

For Jews, this particular Covenant, however understood, cannot be abrogated; it is unbreakable. Jews are judged by a stricter standard than others, but God will never put them utterly aside and find a new love. "I have separated you from other people, that you should be mine." (Lev, 20:222-27) This is both a suffering and a joy, says our great Maimonides, in a letter to suffering Yemenite Jews (Herzberg, 1961. p.27):

> Hold fast to the covenant... Rejoice that you suffer...all for the love of God, to magnify His glorious name. It is the sweetest offering you can make.

Thus the Covenant makes the nearness to God greater; it is not slavery but a way of regular encounter with God. When it is recalled that what is at stake is the encounter with God, then we can recognize that the mode may differ. When the observance becomes slavery, spirit has fled. From a psychological pint of view, the conflict is valuable, as we have said, and it is well to remember that the three competing legs of our triangle are really a dialogue involving God, Jews and Torah, or better yet, a trialogue among Jews, Torah and the World, with God in the center.

I would like to conclude this triangular journey with a Talmudic story. In the second century of our common era, there was a dispute between R. Eliezer and the Sages regarding the ritual purity of an oven. R. Eliezer said, "If the ruling is as I hold, let this carob-tree prove it" and it tore itself out of its place. The Sages declined his demonstration. R. Eliezer continued to demonstrate the truth of his position by causing a stream of water to flow backwards, a wall of a House of Learning to topple, all to no avail. Then a voice from Heaven was heard, which said: "Why do you dispute with R. Eliezer, seeing that in all matters the law is in accord with his ruling?"

The Sages replied: "It is not in Heaven—the Torah states, 'After the majority must one incline' and this means that the law must be decided by majority of human judges and no appeal to a heavenly voice is valid." The story then concludes when Rabbi Nathan met Elijah the Prophet who said that the Lord, when he heard the Sages, laughed and said with joy: "My sons have defeated Me, My sons have defeated Me!" (Talmud, Bava Metzia 59b)

We must conclude that the Lord wants us to obey and to question, to submit and to quarrel. In our triangular struggle, as long as we listen to the voice of the Lord, we are doing what He asks.

> The fateful decision confronting every Jew is therefore not: Shall I or shall I not come under the covenant? but: Shall I affirm my covenant-existence and live an authentic life or shall I deny it and as a consequence live an inauthentic one? Judaism is the living out of the affirmative decision. It is the decision to take the way of the Torah. (Will Herzberg, in Siegel, 1977, p.163)

I would only add that the manner in which one understands this Way is diverse among Jews. Finally, for this decision, one is alone with God, the Author and partner of the original agreement.

It is plain to us all that the trinity of Orthodox, Reform and Conservative does not exhaust the variety of Jewish viewpoints which have flourished in the twentieth century. These three, however different, are agreed in their adherence to the divine principle and to the affirmation of Covenant. We now turn to three other powerful expressions of the Jewish spirit in our century which, although also positive in many ways, carry their power through negation. I am referring to the Ultra-Orthodox, who continue to affirm the Jewish religion but negate the most significant flower of twentieth-century Jewish life, namely Israel. The other two movements have moved away from religion altogether: Marxism, which embraced atheism, and psychoanalysis, which embraced science.

As a representative of the small, though powerful, Ultra-Orthodox, we can appreciate the figure of the Satmar Rebbe, Joel Teitelbaum (Jewish Encyclopedia, pp. 908-910). An illustrious member of a family of Hassidic *zaddikim* and rabbis of Hungary and Galicia going back more than two hundred years, he was saved from the Holocaust and headed the Neturei Karta community in Jerusalem, although he ultimately settled in New York. By means of his scholarship and forceful personality, in writings, sermons and demonstrations, he was one of the most vigorous opponents of Zionism and the State of Israel. To Rabbi Teitelbaum, not only was the way of life— the social and political order in Israel—contrary to *Halakhah*, but the very formation of the state has delayed the coming of the Messiah and the complete redemption of the Jewish people. He went so far as to claim that all the trouble of the Jews in the twentieth century, including the Holocaust, was a punishment for the sins of Zionism and the establishment of a secular state. The use of Hebrew as a spoken language has secularized the holy tongue, as well, To live in Israel was acceptable, but he enjoined his followers to cooperate in no way with its institutions, and in particular not to take the oath of loyalty. He and other Ultra-Orthodox have even given aid and comfort to the enemies of Israel, preferring to live under projected Arab rule.

How can one find anything positive in this, apparently fanatic, negation of that which has united Jews everywhere, Israel, and given them the sense of pride and redemption which was so sorely needed, particularly after the horrors of the Shoah? We can do so, in my opinion, by realizing that this Hassidic Rebbe is not only negating, but affirming. He is expressing the age-old commitment of the people to the Messiah, for the coming of redemption through God and not through man. He is risking all, in a non-religious age, on the link with the divine principle. It is our modest *Halakhic* life and devotion that will bring God to redeem us with *Moshiach* (the Messiah) not our *chutzpah* of grandiosity. Furthermore, we must remember that the Satmar Rebbe belongs to the mystical, Hassidic tradition, going back to the Ba'al Shem Tov and, before that, to the Kabbalistic mysteries. Without this passionate and mystical path to God, Judaism is sorely bereft and can be seen as in danger of being overtaken by dryness and mere observance. Luckily, there are other Hassidim and mystics who are far from negating Israel, but this view, this lonely affirmation of Jewish aloneness, must have a voice. It is more modestly expressed by another Hassid (Patai, 1977, p.197) who said: "God, do not tell me why I suffer, for I am no doubt unworthy to know why, but help me to believe that I suffer for your sake."

As an opposite to this God-centered position, we can readily turn to another scion of a long line of rabbis, Karl Marx, who, in a 1842 letter to Arnold Ruge, admitted that "the Israelite faith" was "repugnant" to him (Patai, 1977, p. 470). We are well aware that for Marx all religion was the "opium of the people," but listen to some quotes from him in his paper "On the Jewish question" (Marx, 1975, pp. 235-241):

> Let us consider the real secular Jew—not the Sabbath Jew...but the everyday Jew. Let us not look for the Jew's secret in his religion: rather let us look for the secret of religion in the real Jew. What is the secular basis of Judaism? Practical need, self-interest. What is the secular cult of the Jew? Haggling. What is his secular god? Money. Well then! Emancipation from haggling and from money, i.e. from practical, real Judaism would be the same as the self-emancipation of our age. An organization of society that abolished the basis upon which haggling exists, i.e. the possibility of haggling, would have made the Jew impossible. (p.236-7)
>
> The Jew has emancipated himself in a Jewish way not only by acquiring financial power but also because through him and apart from him money has become a world power and the practical spirit of the Christian peoples. The Jews have emancipated themselves in so far as the Christians have become Jews (p.237).
>
> Money is the jealous god of Israel before whom no other god may stand. Money debases all the gods of mankind and turns them into commodities... The god of the Jews has been secularized and become the god of the world. (Thus has Judaism attained, through Christianity) world domination, turn(ing) alienated man and alienated nature into alienable, salable objects subject to the slavery of egoistic need and to the market (pp. 240-241).

With such a spokesperson, Jews hardly need any other enemies. But before we vomit with horror at this outpouring of venom, we need to remember that there were many Jews, even scholars (Patai, 1977, p.470) of Marx's time who had internalized gentile stereotypes that Jews were hypocrites, cowards, full of vices and morally depraved. Even those who affirmed Judaism in some aspects, such as the historian Graetz (Graetz, 1949, Vol. 3), vilified it in others, such as in mysticism. Marx knew better than to agree with the notion that all Jews were capitalist exploiters, since he was well-acquainted with the impoverishment of many Jews of his day, but it suited his purposes, it seems, to both revile his ancestors and, at the same time, show that the Christians were no better. It was all a result of the worship of money, he said; human beings had been alienated from themselves because of capitalism.

If we can bracket out, for the moment, his sickening self-hate, we can see that he was indeed aiming to carry out the ancient Jewish goal of bringing about justice and repair of the world. He just left out God. Marx, perhaps unconsciously, did not speak of the "Sabbath Jew," which he did not understand, but of the secular Jew. Nor did he grasp the basis upon which this repair of the world is grounded. He remonstrated like a prophet, but forgot that man is meant to be co-creator with God. Hear our esteemed Soloveitchik on this point (Soloveitchik, 1983, p.107):

> Man is obliged to perfect what his Creator [left] impaired... The Jewish people bring a sacrifice to atone, as it were, for the Holy One, blessed be He, for not having completed the work of creation. The Creator of the world diminished the image and stature of creation in order to leave something for man, the work of His hands, to do, in order to adorn man with the crown of creator and maker.

When I remember the passionate rendering of the communist Internationale in the 1930's, with its call: "Arise ye prisoners of starvation; arise ye wretched of the earth" and how powerfully it gripped so many, I am heartened by the following quotation from Soloveitchik, which expresses the same sentiment. For me, it gives scriptural grounding for that passion and also for what I do as a psychotherapist (Soloveitchik, 1983, p.131):

> The command of creation, beating deep within the consciousness of Judaism, proclaims: Awake ye slumberers from your sleep. Realize, actualize yourselves, your own potentialities and possibilities, and go forth to meet your God. The unfolding of man's spirit that soars to the very heavens, that is the meaning of creation.

Marx belonged to that group of emancipated Jews of whom Bernard Lazare (1865-1903) spoke as "no longer bound by the faith of his ancestors," yet still shaped by the "revolutionary Jewish spirit" and, therefore, "a breeder of revolutions" (Patai, 1977, p. 475). He therefore was in the good company of such emancipated Jews as Heine and Disraeli. The latter, at least, were free of the self-hate that Marx represented. Since the Holocaust and the establishment of Israel, thank goodness, that poison has diminished to the vanishing point.

When we consider the tremendous chasm between the deep theism of the Ultra-Orthodox and the atheism of the Marxists, we become aware that the division we saw earlier, between the Orthodox and Reform, is expanded greatly. But just as the Conservative position arose to mediate the former opposites, another third position came in to mediate between Jewish particularists and Jewish deniers. I am referring to that loosely labeled "humanist" position to which many Jews subscribe, affirming the value of Jewish history and culture, but rejecting the religious aspects altogether. Such people constitute significant numbers in both Israel and the Diaspora and themselves fill a large spectrum between Yiddishists and merely "gastronomic" Jews. Chiefly, they seem to be adherents of Jewish culture but embrace a scientific, enlightened viewpoint which believes that religion is as necessary for people as a fish needs a bicycle.

An outstanding adherent of this viewpoint is Sigmund Freud, a man as influential in the non-Jewish world as was Marx. In his well-known book, *Moses and Monotheism* (Freud, 1939, vol. 23), Freud indulged his fantasy that Moses was an Egyptian, but the great psychologist did not reject his people while trying to understand them. He speaks of the Jewish character, as follows (Freud, vol. 23, p. 106):

> There is no doubt that they have a particularly high opinion of themselves, that they regard themselves as superior to other peoples—from whom they are also distinguished by their customs. At the same time they are inspired by a peculiar confidence in life, such as is derived from the secret ownership of some precious possession, a kind of optimism; pious people would call it trust in God. We know the reason for this behavior and what their secret treasure is. They really regard themselves as God's chosen people, they believe that they stand especially close to him and this makes them proud and confident. (Freud, 1939, p.134).

Although seeming to share this pride and confidence, Freud's non-religious attitude does not include observance and, as is well-known, adherence to the law he attributes merely to guilt, which was insatiable and came from sources much deeper; they must make those commandments grow ever stricter, more meticulous and even more trivial.

The man who could never understand the "oceanic feeling" might not be expected to understand *Halakhic* man either. Luckily, there are other depth-psychologists who do grasp the basis of religious experience, so we are not limited in our appreciation of the unconscious to Freud's view, just as we are not limited in our grasp of socialism to the atheistic position of Marx.

But Freud, unlike Marx, did not reject his Jewish roots; on the contrary, he valued them. In an address to the Society of B'nai B'rith, he said (Patai, 1977, p.379):

> What bound me to Jewry was (I am ashamed to say) neither faith nor national pride... But plenty of other things remained over to make the attraction of Jewry and Jews irresistible—many obscure emotional forces, which were the more powerful the less they could

be expressed in words, as well as a clear consciousness of an inner identity, the safe privacy of a common mental construction. And beyond this, there was a perception that it was to my Jewish nature alone that I owed two characteristics that had become indispensable to me in the difficult course of my life. Because I was a Jew I found myself free from many prejudices which restricted others in the use of their intellect; and as a Jew I was prepared to join the Opposition and to do without agreement with the 'compact majority.'

He could not know, as have others since then, that he, like all of us, had other unconscious prejudices, but he, along with Einstein and so many other "modern" Jews, contributed whole new viewpoints, vistas and understandings to the larger world. If they abandoned their God-given role of Jewish priest and witness to God, this priesthood has devolved into the modern world perspective of science.

Now, having traversed these six different viewpoints among modern Jews, it remains for us to attempt some integration of them, using our modern phenomenological and psychological understanding. The first fact which confronts us is the ever-present existence of conflict—between believers and non-believers, followers and non-followers of *Halakha*, rationalists and mystics. This condition of opposition and conflict was built-in, so to speak; it is not only characteristic of the psyche of *Halakhic* man, as Rabbi Soloveitchik informed us, but has been discovered, by C.G. Jung, to be the basis upon which the psyche as a whole is built up. Here is how Soloveitchik beautifully described this condition (Soloveitchik, 1983, p.107):

> Man himself symbolizes, on the one hand, the most perfect and complete type of existence, the image of God, and on the other hand, the most terrible chaos and void to reign over creation. [This endless dualism] sets the entire task of creation and the obligation to participate in the renewal of the cosmos. The most fundamental principle of all is that man must create himself. It is this idea that Judaism introduced into the world.

This quotation would be heartily endorsed by Jung, I think, except that he would opine that in the chaos also resides the divine principle. His concept of individuation, translated from psychological terms, is equivalent to Soloveitchik's "man must create himself." And Freud would certainly agree with the main idea of self-creation, although leaving God out. Our other antagonists would also embrace this view, so surely Soloveitchik is right in attributing this conflict to the Jewish psyche itself.

But there are other oppositions within our groups not so easily reconciled. For example, there is the conflict between the longing for the God who transcends all, the *Ein Sof* of the mystics, versus Soloveitchik speaking about the ritual symbolism of the ram's horn and of the divine significance of the fruits of this world (p.62):

> The sounding of the *shofar* represents the yearning for the *Deus Absconditus* whom no thought can grasp... The *shofar* weeps... over the infinite distance that separates the cosmos from the *Ein-Sof*, the infinite God. Therefore, it negates the world and raises man to the most absolute transcendent mode of existence. In contrast, the taking of the *lulav* and the *etrog*—the fruit of a goodly tree—sustains and affirms the beautiful and resplendent world, which reflects the glory of the God who fills and encompasses all worlds.

Basic, therefore, to the whole ground of Judaism, this duality exists from the outset, in the two trees of Paradise, and is seen in the quarrel between Hillel and Shammai. The former was anthropocentric, focusing on the love of man; the latter was theocentric, centering on the fear of God and obedience to Him. Both men, of course, sought to raise the standards of human conduct in order that the glory of God would be "most clearly manifest on earth."

The duality is also seen even in one of the chief virtues of the Jewish people, namely charity or *tzedakah*. Hear what Rabbi Abba bar Aha said about the Jews (Hertzberg, 1961, p.30):

> One cannot determine the nature of this people. When asked to contribute for making the golden calf, they give; when asked to contribute for constructing the Tabernacle, they give.

Nor is this people merely receptive or rebellious to the admonitions from on high. Not infrequently does the opposition appear to be guilt-making of the deity, himself—respectfully of course, but nonetheless there. Listen, for example, to Reb Mayerl, *tzaddik* of Przemyslany, Galicia, who argued with God (Patai, 1977, p.201):

> Are You not ashamed of Yourself, Master of the World? You created man of flesh and blood, of such weak stuff, and made him susceptible to every sin, whereas You should have created him strong and steadfast so that nothing should sway him; then You let him sin, although You could have safeguarded him from it—and now, on top of everything, You punish him? Are You not ashamed of Yourself?

That this is not a unique criticism can be seen from the statement of Rabbi Elimelekh of Lizhensk who sent disciples to observe a tailor at prayer on the Day of Atonement. The tailor was overheard to say: "I will forgive You for Your sins (Lord), if You will forgive me for mine." It was reported that God Himself and His heavenly court had come to listen to the tailor and his words caused great joy in all spheres. Clearly, the priesthood and partnership are seen as mutually interlacing. "Man the creature, is commanded to become a partner with the Creator in the renewal of the cosmos; complete and ultimate creation—this is the deepest desire of the Jewish people." (Soloveitchik, 1983, p.105)

We can now visualize our six Jewish viewpoints in terms of our two triangles, as we have suggested, and join them together into a single Star of David, interlacing, intersecting and uniting into one. We can see them clearly as the many corners of Jewish attitude, but can we also see them as aspects of all of us? Are we not all, to some degree, partners to the Covenant, searchers for freedom, honoring of tradition, waiting for the Messiah, asserting the repair of the world, seeing the roots of our being in psyche and world? And are we not, on the shadow side, also rigid and fundamentalist, wishy-washy and assimilative, fanatic and rootless, prejudiced and arrogant? The Jewish psyche is also our individual Jewish psyches, I think, and it would be helpful if each of us recognized the divergent views as aspects of one's self as well.

If these opposites complement and balance each other, there is a wholeness; if not, there is chaos and horror. Kabbalah tells us that the source of evil is the imbalance of the *Sephirot* on the Tree of Life; Justice without Mercy, or Power without Love are productive of evil, as is the reverse. Indeed, great Evil itself is a consequence of one of the *Sephirot* detaching itself from the harmonious Tree and arrogating to itself a total apartness. For Jews, relationship is everything. We are even told in Kabbalah (Patai, 1977, p.87) that without Israel, God cannot be whole. Change and development are all part of this, and our very survival is due to the will of God. Isaiah (6:13) tells us that the great oak of Israel must cast off its leaves, but its holy seed must grow back into a new stock.

If we can also recognize that in the center of the interlocking triangles is a single point which can be seen as the *Shekhina*, expressing a feminine side of God, then we can better grasp the ancient view (Hertzberg, 1961, p.148), that the exile of the Jews is also the exile of the *Shekhina* and is thus a suffering of God. Again: without Israel, says Kabbalah, not even God can be whole.

We can best close with a quote from Jonah ben Landsofer (1678-1712), a Bohemian Talmudist whose last will said (Hertzberg, 1961,p.225):

> The first thing that should be said is the great principle that the purpose of the creation of man is the service of God. The essential part of this service is in man's innermost being and the heart watches over it.

If we allow that God speaks to us individually and deeply—we are all priests of God—we can grant that the very multiplicity we witness is God's experimentation with His and our nature. The *Shema* ("Hear O Israel! The Lord our God is One") is both our truth and our goal.

REFERENCES

Freud, Sigmund (1939). *Moses And Monotheism*. Collected Works, edited by J. Strachey, Vol. 23

Graetz, Heinrich (1949). *History Of The Jews* (six volumes,. Hebrew Publishing Company, New York. (original 1888 and 1849)

Hertzberg, Arthur (1961). Editor, *Judaism,*. Prentice Hall International, London. 256 pp.

Jewish Encyclopedia

Jung, C.G. (1952 ff) *Collected Works*, 20 volumes.

Marx, Karl (1975). *Early Writings*., Vintage Books, New York.

Patai, Raphael (1977). *The Jewish Mind.*, Charles Scribner's Sons, New York. 624 pp.

Siegel, Seymour (1977). Editor, *Conservative Judaism And Jewish Law,*. The Rabbinical Assembly, New York. 337 pp.

Soloveitchik, Rabbi Joseph B. (1983). *Halakhic Man,*. Jewish Publication Society of America, Philadelphia. 164 pp. (originally published in 1944).

Van der Leeuw, Gerhard (1938). *Religion In Essence And Manifestation.*, George Allen and Unwin. London. 709 pp.

A JEWISH PSYCHOTHERAPIST LOOKS AT THE RELIGIOUS FUNCTION OF THE PSYCHE

(For the Conference of the Association of Orthodox Jewish Scientists, UCLA, Los Angeles, March 5, 1989)

Among the founders of depth psychology at the beginning of this century, it was only C.G. Jung who observed that a religious function was natural to the psyche and that if this internal necessity was not fulfilled in some way, neurosis was likely to occur. This was particularly important for the second half of life, he felt, after the individual had somehow come to grips with the normal human problems of adaptation to the world in terms of career and family. Freud had clearly seen the fundamental importance to the psyche of sexuality and early upbringing and Adler had outlined the significance of power and social interest, but neither saw religion as an inner necessity. Rather, their observations led them to think that religious training and attitudes might lead to neurosis. The latter view was supported further by the work of later psychoanalysts, such as Wilhelm Reich, who found that the rigidity of body armoring and the horrors of emotional plague could be laid at the door of instinct-denying religious training. Aside from Jung, then, depth psychology has not been exactly friendly to the religious attitude.

Now, a century since the beginning of depth psychotherapy, we may be able to ascertain whether there is, indeed, a religious function of the mind, as Jung maintained, or whether this is merely an outgrowth of more primitive ways of dealing with psyche and world, as other psychoanalysts believed. One way of doing this is for psychotherapists who have engaged in this work to report on their own experiences. Those who have been compelled to take people's problems as they arise and to follow processes of psychological development would presumably be in a position to say something useful along these lines.

At one level, it is puerile to even raise the question of whether religion is important for the human psyche, since it is evident that every culture known has had some form of worship or relationship to higher powers. Even the Marxist nations are finding that the failure of their utopian vision requires an adaptation not only to capitalist ways of dealing with the

21

economy, but also allowing the powerful forces of national, tribal and religious identity to resume their place in those countries where these have been repressed. Such social trends, however, do not force us to conclude that the religious function must be fulfilled by all individuals. People in psychological trouble, at least those who come to psychotherapists, may demonstrate this more effectively.

What of my own religious orientation? I grew up in a fairly assimilated, non-observant, Jewish household, although I went to a Talmud-Torah during my grade-school years and enjoyed a traditional bar-mitzvah under the watchful eye of my ancient and highly religious grandfather. I had spiritual interests from childhood onwards and, after the customary Marxist rebellion of my early adolescence, gravitated to all sorts of spiritual reading. My first analysis, in my twenties, awakened deeper spiritual issues for me and I had a number of religious experiences which were crucial for my life. My basic therapeutic struggles, however, had to do with the usual working through of childhood, and of relationship and career. It was only my later training analysis in Zurich, in my early thirties, which provided me sufficient time, spiritual support, and information which made possible the kind of process that Jung describes, say, in his second of the "Two Essays," where one systematically relates to the psyche itself, internalizes the contra-sexual images and arrives at a relativization of the ego and a relationship to the Self, the central authority of the soul which carries a divine imprint. That was not unusual among my fellow students—a deep process of that nature was even expected. That few of us were even permitted by the Swiss government to hold jobs made it possible to devote total energy to this attention to the soul. As a consequence, these profound experiences, like those undergone by religious seekers historically, became possible.

Just as what happens at the cultural level does not necessarily prove or disprove what occurs at the individual level, we have to recognize that what takes place in the practice of individual therapy does not necessarily reflect what is happening in the larger milieu. A general reportage, however, of therapists from a variety of backgrounds and experiences might enhance our understanding of this issue and help us sort out where we psychotherapists are as we, in our solitude, approach the end of one hundred years of depth psychology. The following reflections, then, constitute the beginning of such a reportage from a Jewish psychotherapist who is religious in attitude, although not traditionally observant.

What, then, have I learned about the presence of a religious function in the psyche during almost forty years of immersion in the problems and souls of people who have undergone psychotherapy or analysis? The answer is not so easy to give, since it seems to depend upon the day I think about this issue. The day after I felt that not much of a religious nature was happening with my patients, I was asked to do this paper and several patients, theretofore non-religious, came up with profound dreams or experiences of a religious nature! As a religious man and as a Jungian Analyst, I of course took this as a synchronistic event and a numinous reply to my implied question.

If I think of the clergy and consciously religious people I have worked with over the years, as well as the spiritually advanced souls who have participated in profound processes, there is no doubt about the religious function of the psyche. Yet many of the people I have seen have not felt the need to take up religious issues. Rather, their interest and concern have centered upon the traditional loci of relationship and career or, as Freud specified as the most important aspects of life, love and work. Their struggles have been with parental imagos, with power issues—a la Adler—such as success and failure in all areas of life. Does this mean that the answer to our question has to do primarily with the nature of the person asking it and the particular population that he/she addresses? Apparently so. But, since I am religious and have encountered opposite kinds of experiences, what does this mean? The answer seems to require a deeper and more differentiated response to what religion means, and it is in this direction that I now intend to proceed.

Few people in the rush of American life have either the possibility of desire to become a kind of modern-day anchorite, or even a totally God-centered seeker. Rather, the contents of the psyche of a deeply archetypal or religious nature arise, but not in such profusion or with such an all-absorbing character. Perhaps this is just as well: it is usually better to undergo such a process only when there is a deep need or even necessity; the danger of psychosis or other separation from ordinarily life is too great. So, the fact that there are people in ordinary life in the United States who have such experiences while continuing to live their lives with family and work, is remarkable in itself. One might even speculate that this sort of process is particularly important for one who seeks to become a Jungian Analyst, so that he/she can understand and be helpful to those who do undergo such a process, but that this is not essential for the large majority of patients.

Does this mean that religious experience is a function like intelligence and that it varies considerably among the population according to need and capacity? The answer may appear to be yes, but I think that something else is afoot, and before we answer, we need to better define what we mean by religion.

Jung understood the word, religion, in terms of its derivation from the Latin, *religio*, which refers to the careful observation of those events and conditions of life which are "numinous," which contain an element of the awe-inspiring, the *tremendum* and *mysterium*, as described by Rudolf Otto. Jung felt that these experiences of the Other, of the transcendent and deeply moving, were characteristic of the psyche, and that these aspects of the mind could be observed and connected with. Indeed, were one to embark upon a long-term study of one's dreams and fantasies, the expectation would be that such experiences would take place and one could thereby know for oneself that the divine is a fundamental and formative quality within and behind one's own soul. In a sense, Jung would agree with those historical figures who said that the soul is "naturally religious." This understanding of the religious attitude and function, as located within the psyche itself, is to be contrasted with the other derivation of the word, religion, which is *religare*, meaning to "bind back." This is more in line with that understanding of religion which links it to group belief, attitude and ritual—we are thereby "bound back" to our origins in the divine and to the group of which we are a part. This latter derivation is more in line with the normative Jewish understanding of religion, as a question of right practice and behavior. Hasting's *Dictionary of the Bible*, for example, says the following about religion (p.841):

> The word 'religion,' where it occurs (in the Bible), signifies not the inner spirit of the religious life, but its outward expression.

Thus the normative concerns of Judaism, as with Islam and Christianity as well, have to do with right action or behavior. Yet we also know that any world religion must also address the inner spiritual aspects, as does Jewish mysticism, for example. A depth psychological focus, naturally, will usually center more on experience than behavior. Jung's attention to the psyche and its experiences has more in common with the writings of mystical Judaism, such as Kabbalah.

These two approaches, that of behavior and experience, are to be found in differing degree among all the great religions. They do not necessarily have to be in conflict, although they sometimes are. My own perspective is that both are necessary in some sense. Jung's famous "individuation" requires being alone with one's own soul and its contents, yet to be only alone is to risk being cut off from one's fellows and community and thereby suffer a consequent alienation. On the other hand, it was the great Rabbi Joseph Soloveitchik who spoke about the "loneliness" of the observant Jew, the separating experience of the power of the divine when one celebrates the *mitzvoth*.

The fact is that people can be alone with their psyches and fail to have numinous experiences, or at least to see them that way, although they may suffer terribly the vicissitudes of life. And the correlative fact is that people may practice mitzvoth or other religious ritual without experiencing much of anything numinous. Spirituality, or the attention to the transcendent, with consequent experience, is independent of both of these activities, yet one engages in them partly with the hope or expectation that the divine will enter into them.

Now, how does this apply to psychotherapy? In analysis, patients surely attend to their dreams and fantasies, associate to them, interpret them. Some, although not many, even engage in Jung's famous method of active imagination, the conscious relationship to fantasy which, when undertaken over along period, does lead to the experiences that he speaks about in his second essay. Yet few persist in this process, at least to the extent that is required to arrive at the phenomenology of the Self about which Jung writes. Most analysands have dreams and fantasies, however, and these do reveal the archetypal nature of the psyche. "Mother" is often not just mother, but is also experienced as the Great Mother, terrible and wonderful, and far beyond what our personal and mortal mother's capacity really is. Furthermore, the child in us that is at the center of one's interest and suffering often turns out to be the "hero" or even the "divine" child, with qualities far beyond ordinary infantility. The same can be said for all the other archetypal factors which underlie the routine images of life and give them their powerful impact. But any Freudian analyst can tell you that one can speak of omnipotence and use such words as the "paranoid position," when referring to transcendence, and not have the divine in mind at all! That is where the reductive attitude of Freud comes in, and where Jung had to part company. Nowadays, there are other therapists who give worth to the religious attitude, such as Frankl, but none have surpassed Jung in the mapping of the psyche in such a way as to describe its multi-leveled religious qualities.

The crucial fact in all this is that much of the material that turns up in psychotherapy or analysis, called oral or anal or phallic, or narcissistic or omnipotent, etc. are terms really referring to archetypal figures and events. Myth is at the core of the psyche; even Freud recognized one of them, the Oedipus story, and made it the center of his system. Jung discovered that the modern psyche is heavily engaged in continuing what medieval alchemy was involved in, but carries other names, such as those used by psychoanalysts. The transformation of one's own psyche, the struggle with instinctive strivings, with conscience, with the problems of love and lust, power and compassion, is the daily fare of what we do, yet most do not see this as religious, or even spiritual.

How do we account for this fact? Is it simply that the religious man perceives in religious categories and the agnostic does not? That surely has more than a grain of truth in it. Yet we also know that the experience of the divine can have a most powerful impact and change a person's beliefs in a hurry. I think, now, of an atheistic Jewish professional man I once worked with, who said, after the birth of his first child:

Before my child was born, I looked around at the world and it was obvious that there was no God. Now, I look at my child and it is obvious that there is!

But I could also quote other people whose work on their own souls leads them to reject the religion of their origin. My own experience however, is in accord with Jung. Over his door he had the saying engraved, "Summoned or not, God is always present." The names change, become "isms" or passions, but the soul's experiences of powers which compel it, dwarf it, sustain it, do contain that sense of the *religio* I have mentioned earlier. Whether one puts such experiences into psychoanalytic categories or alchemical categories or traditional religious categories seems not to matter too much to the deeper soul which is being affected. The effect is all and it seems to be our human task to somehow work this out. Religious tradition and imagery, since it speaks the language of the soul in greatest depth and variety, is most helpful when one finally transcends the limited personalistic aspects of existence and addresses the transpersonal.

Those who undertake the spiritual path via their own psyches are deeply enriched thereby, but often continue to be alienated from community, spiritual and otherwise. Those who do not undertake such a path may be comfortable in their community yet may not experience the psychic reality of what their religious customs and rituals point to. Happy is the person who can combine both! This was the condition of human beings, generally, before the modern "enlightenment;" it is the latter which has compelled the centuries-long re-examination, from an independent scientific and spiritual viewpoint, of all consciousness, including the religious. We are slowly finding our way, back and forward, to a union of a critical spirit with the religious one.

At this point, I would like to illustrate my remarks by examining dreams from Jewish people, all but two of which came to my attention within a few weeks of my being asked to present this paper. It is as if my question was posed as to the religious function of the psyche, and the answer came in the dreams of several patients and others. Those dreamers I report on, may be considered to have been essentially agnostic, which is crucial for our question. A consideration of such dreams may reveal some intent on the part of the unconscious and, perhaps, can give us a clue as to what is afoot in all this.

The first dream comes from a man in his mid-forties, in the arts, successful, in analysis for his development. Jewish religion and community have meant very little to him ever since he had his bar mitzvah and found the experience meaningless. This dream occurs after a couple of years of analysis and he has gradually gone deeper into his own psyche. He calls it "Jew's Dream":

> I play, as when I was a boy. My sword thrusts out from my hand, extension of my arm, of my manliness still to come. I am 16 or so (nearly three decades ago). I thrust and dance, hopping about like some adolescent Quixote in search of an imaginary foe. But I am not

on the ground. Instead, I am atop a rubble. The remains of a building, of a large house. Here and there, some framing still stands, skeleton of a house that once filled all this space and encompassed it. There was a home of some kind here, but home to whom, or what? What was a kind of brightness all around in the beginning has now changed. The lighting is now warmer, redder, as sky that has seen fire. I am atop the rubble that is still warm, but is a fallen and burned house.

To my left and behind me there is a man. A Jew. He wears a suit and hat and a *talis* and carries the daily prayer book in his hands. I do not see him because he is slightly beyond my periphery, but I know he is there and I know what he looks like except that I do not know his face. I don't need to. He is the Jew of the synagogue and I do not trust him or feel close to him in any way. He is the stranger to whom my parents have entrusted me, in the synagogue, where I study to be a Jew without knowing what that means. Except that *I feel* what it is to be a Jew. Outsider. So *that* is what I feel in common with him...that we are a congregation of exiles. Small comfort, this camaraderie. If it comes down to life or death, he will save himself before me.

Suddenly, before me, appears an older man, with the face of an aging character actor of whom I am fond. An actor, by the way, who is a Jew. This older man, not feeble, but old nonetheless, is stooped a little, and I respect him. I esteem him. I love him because his wisdom protects me somehow. He acknowledges me, smiles, with his mouth and his eyes and his whole face. I have no sword now, only a *talis* that clings to my shoulders. When I was a boy, I loved the feel of the *talis* around me; smooth and silky and cool, fringed with those wonderful threads that ran through and around my fingers...

The old man extends his arms towards me and I bend toward him. The ends of the *talis* are locked in the fingers of each of my hands, left and right. Slowly, in balance and harmony, I arc the talis over my head so that it shelters me like a tent. Then I draw my arms down and wrap myself in its folds.

A great sob rises up from inside me and heaves itself out of my heart and out of my mouth and I shudder. My shoulders rock with the truth of it: *I am a Jew.*

Though I have lost that nearer God, the One who stands close by and unseen, still I know inside the *talis* that I am a Jew. And in the embrace of the old man I am home for the first time in many years. Among the people. Kinship felt. Tribal. Family beyond my own. A greater family. Enduring. Perhaps even to be trusted in time of dire need.

I weep with joy and sadness that I am home and that I have been away. The Jew of the congregation, to my left and behind me, he is not to be trusted. But the old man, the Jew of the Ages, I trust him, because I am his future and he cherishes me and will protect me. I am home at last. Weary, spent, safe, I rest. (End of dream.)

This dream, touching and eloquent, needs little interpretation. We need only observe that, after a couple of years of struggle, this alienated Jew unexpectedly finds his way back to his people in a new initiation, now under the *talis*, the "tent" of us all. He is linked through art and common fate, but is both suspicious of the fully observant Jew and is still somewhat distant from that "nearer God, the one who stands close by and unseen." But this is less than mid-way through his process, still unfolding. I make special note here of the initial condition of being "atop a rubble." The spiritual home of the dreamer has been destroyed, but the sky that "has seen fire" is "now warmer, redder." This hint of the destruction of our people and the possibility of renewal is made even clearer by the dream of our second person.

This dreamer, approaching his ninetieth year, has never had any analysis and is far from having any psychological interest. He is strongly Jewish, ethnically, but does not feel any particular religious concern, having "escaped" from the narrow religiosity of a boyhood in Poland. He enjoys a zestful life, however, and, if there is a God, he says, he would prefer to stay out of His sight. Yet, some years ago, during an unusual episode of illness, he dreamed as follows:

He finds himself in the forests of his boyhood in Poland and is deeply affected by the intense green and beauty. Then he is somewhere else in Europe and it is after the Holocaust. Everywhere he looks there is only destruction. Only small stones and bits of human objects are visible—a complete rubble. Then he sees only one thing that is undamaged: a small stand upon which the Torah normally rests on the *bimah*.

At that moment he sees and hears great numbers of youth, who are now coming to rebuild once more. (End of dream.)

These two dreams reflect all too clearly the great calamity which has come upon the Jewish people, destruction from without and loss of connection with God from within. Yet the souls of these two men, neither one consciously seeking religious experience or affiliation, suggests to us that the psyche is, indeed, "naturally religious." Neither man has changed his outer behavior as a result of these dreams, yet can we doubt that something profound has happened, is happening, and will continue to happen?

The psychotherapist does not figure large on the world scene, but he does have the privilege of seeing how the soul is participating in the great social and religious transformations of our time. Lest you think, however, that such dreams occur only to people in psychotherapy or to relatives of Jungian Analysts, let me quote another dream, recently revealed in a Jewish newspaper ("The Jewish Journal," Los Angeles, January 20-26, 1989, p.29) from a man (Christopher Hitchens) who had lived well into adulthood believing himself to be an English Christian and suddenly discovering that his deceased mother was Jewish. He reports that he was "pleased to find that I was pleased" at the tidings, and then recalled a dream that he had some time before in which he was:

> ...aboard a ship. A small group is on the other side of the deck, huddled in talk but in some way noticing myself. After a while, a member of the group crosses the deck. He explains that he and his fellows are one short of a quorum for prayer. Will I make up the number for a *minyan*?? Smiling generously, and swallowing my secular convictions in a likable and tolerant manner, I agree to make up the number and stroll across the deck. (End of dream.)

It is a common saying among Jews that the "Jewish soul knows itself." Indeed, it is said that it longs for realization and this is what accounts for people far removed from Jewish religious life or not even knowing that they are Jewish who respond most powerfully to scenes of *davening*, or prayer. This is far from automatic, of course, since there have been conversions and assimilation away from Judaism through all historical time, without dreams like those mentioned. And yet...the psyche knows something.

I now turn to dreams of two women, neither of whom was particularly religious before undergoing analysis. The first woman, an Israeli, after undergoing some difficult, apparently intractable, problems, dreamt as follows.

> We were sitting in a beautiful place on the Kineret. It was almost evening. There were shadows on the water. Everyone sat on a rock in the water. There was a group of soldiers, among them a commander who talked to each one in a most understanding way. They were full of hardships, "kshei yom." I sat there too, on the rock. Somebody started to sing a beautiful song, the melody and words were magnificent. The refrain of the song was 'Elda, Elda,' meaning, 'God knows it' or 'Know God.' But this was also the name of the commander, which is a masculine form, but the name of a woman. Everyone joined in. The song was new. I felt tears streaming down my face, and everyone else did too, including the commander. His shoulders were shaking as if he was crying. It was

kind of 'thank you' in the form of a song, full of emotion, for his understanding. Then as the song ended, they started to sing it again. I joined in. (End of dream.)

This touching dream suggests the dreamer's contact with what a Jungian would understand as a symbol of the Self, a higher inner authority who connects with the divine. Characteristically, the figure combines male and female in some manner and is both deeply affecting and affected by the dreamer. It of course gave her great solace in her suffering and sense that "God knows" or "Know God."

The second woman dreamer is from North Africa, has had many years of analysis, but the following dream was the first of its kind for her:

I am outside at night. There is a beautiful, very starry sky. I think my father is there, too. Suddenly there is a force of some kind that manifests itself, coming down from heaven, a supernatural energy. I know with certainty that 'this is It.' It is God in a sense, but not the way we usually think of God; it is not so much a 'being.' However, it makes me feel sure of the existence of a Divinity and that I have experienced it. There is now no doubt in my mind. (Some material deleted).

Then we (dreamer and her father) are in a room. I say to him: 'The Messiah will show himself to very prominent people (or rich) or very poor ones, but not to us. We are always left out. Maybe it will not even affect our everyday life; it will not change it. But what if it changes the world? If we have world peace?' I felt wonderful about that and the certainty of the Divine once again. (End of dream.)

This dream merits further discussion, but in or present context I want to report that messianic-type dreams do occur these days—rarely, of course, but with some regularity. Whether they refer to significant psychic changes going on with the dreamers—as they surely do—or also refer to collective events is hard to discern. That theme deserves a paper in itself.

Finally, I want to refer to another incident taking place during these eventful weeks following my being asked to speak to this audience, which illustrates another aspect of our general issue of whether the psyche does have a religious function. In my work with a non-believing Jewish man with good education, it emerged that his great fear of death was associated with the irrational belief that he could control his own mortality. He knew, of course, that such a belief was both irrational and impossible, but it gripped him. For me, this was evidence of the religious function of the psyche, working in a still-confused way with him for reasons not altogether clear. One might say that instead of having a healthy "fear of God" and a capacity to surrender to the presence of the higher power, he was caught with both a morbid fear and an inflated belief in control. Ego and Self were contaminated, from a Jungian point of view. In time, one thinks that the same unconscious which provoked such confusion will present experiences and understanding which will permit him to find a natural religious function and thus free him from the morbid aspects. That is what Jung had in mind, I think, when he wrote that every neurosis beyond middle age ultimately hinged on a religious issue. We all must die, we all must form some relationship to the Other. Many among us, it seems, must also find a religious solution to these events, but whether it is everyone who must do so, I do not know.

What I can say, however, is that work with psyche has significant impact on the therapist as well. Some of us feel that we are embroiled in a spiritual process with some analysands; indeed, our work itself is seen as spiritual in nature. We are affected, too. After a session with the aforementioned atheist who feared death and was bedeviled by demons in the night, I myself dreamed of seeing a frightening demon. I whimpered with fear and was awakened by the comforting hand of my wife. I realized that even though I had been supportive of my patient that day, I secretly felt superior to him, in his attitude toward death. The unconscious put me in my place, showing that I, too, was vulnerable and it behooves us all to avoid inflation and realize our own "creatureliness," our smallness in the face of the God who manifests everywhere in life, including the human soul, yet goes beyond whatever categories we apply in our efforts to understand, to worship, and to be whole.

STRUGGLING WITH THE IMAGE OF GOD

(Conference on Psychology and Judaism at Cedars-Sinai Hospital Los
Angeles, California, March 9, 1986)

When Rabbi Meier invited my participation in this conference, he had
tentatively entitled it Tradition and Autonomy in Judaism. My reflections
on the theme of these psychological opposites led me to the conclusion that
Conscience was one place where they met. I had planned to center my
remarks on this when a reminder of the conference came to me with the
title now transformed into "Conscience and Autonomy in Judaism." I let
the synchronicity stand as a validation of my conclusion, but now I saw that
the implied conflict between collective and individual was being softened.
All the better, then, that my theme of "struggling with the image of God"
would continue the aspect of conflict, since there is indeed, an implied
possibility of opposition between these two aspects of religious life, without
which creative innovation would be impossible.

So, then, my topic is the interplay of Tradition and Autonomy, one
aspect of which can be seen as the "struggle with the image of God." By
this I mean that every religion and every person has an image of God,
conscious or unconscious, and that this image changes with time,
experience and development. Every world religion, furthermore, has within
itself significant elements which nourish both a collective and an individual
encounter with the divine. This would have to be true since we know, from
a psychological point of view, that both dimensions are deeply imbedded in
the nature of the psyche itself and constitute the fundamental basis upon
which the individuation process proceeds. Without our general humanity
and its particular expression in the traditions into which we are born, we are
not even human. And without our personal uniqueness,—a product of the
concatenation of genes and environment, nature and nurture—that
generality would be unremarkable. Religion, indeed, celebrates and
dramatizes both aspects and provides a vehicle by which we can both
recognize and participate in our communality via ritual and belief. It also
gives us a structure in which our personal experiences of the divine can be
both evoked and meaningfully explained.

When all goes well, there is no breach between individual and
collective and a seamless web joins the two. This is true even when there is
religious struggle, for example, between desire and the law. The resultant

33

conflict, experienced by the person, can readily remain in the context of religious practice and eventuate in both deepened appreciation and more meaningful observance.

But what about when things do not go well? How is it when a person can no longer believe in or observe all the tenets of his or her faith, yet does not find himself/herself in rebellion? Or, even more to the point, what happens when a person has religious experiences, even experiences of God, which do not fit into the revealed expectations of the tradition? Is he/she to abandon these experiences as heretical? Should one—as is common— merely "demonize" these experiences as being outside of tradition and therefore false? Or can one struggle with these experiences, undergo within one's self the agonizing containment of the strife of the opposites, hoping and praying for the grace which will provide a solution?

The latter mode is found in many creative persons in the religions and, indeed, is presented as a model in the founders themselves. Jesus, for example, is crucified, literally and figuratively, by being both divine and mortal, God and man, and undergoes an unspeakable suffering of these opposites, finally showing a way to his followers to find the Christ in themselves. The Kingdom of God lies within you, he repeatedly said. Yet these same followers may suffer a confusion in their *imitatio Christi*, whether to follow his example of embracing their own divinity and humanity, or to only follow a traditional pattern.

In Buddhism, we are given the extraordinarily potent symbol of the Buddha sitting at the base of the Bo tree, asserting that he will not rise until he is enlightened, subjecting himself to all the gods and demons who assault him. The resultant way to enlightenment, as evidenced in the path of meditation, for example, can bring about an experience of the Self within. But does this realization in the ordinary meditator lead to individuation— particularity and uniqueness—or to another collective image of the "holy man?"

The latter distinction came home to me during my first analysis, when I was less than twenty-five. I had come up against a brick wall of resistance in myself and, when I let this wall speak, following the method of Jung's active imagination, a short poem emerged in Biblical style. Within this cryptic poem, was the following couplet:

> Holy man, hollow man
> Solo man, Soloman.

I understood this couplet to mean that the Holy man was really a hollow man, in both senses of the work: empty, yet possibly pregnant in this emptiness, with a potential fullness of the divine. The second line, however, suggested that the man who stood alone was the wise man, the Soloman. In short, the holy man was empty for me at that time, and I had to find my "holiness"—such as it was—from within myself. At other times, of course, I have had no such need, nor could I recommend this generally. Yet the distinction holds: we can find our religious figures both within ourselves and outside ourselves, and sometimes they are in conflict.

The truly religious person, however, is both encouraged to participate in this inner struggle and enjoined not to become heretical. And this is as it should be, since the collective perforce wants us to continue in it, to treasure its rich and soul-saving past, and to protect us all from the chaos of a non-believing world. These days we are all too clear about the dangers to civilization from those who have no religious commitment at all. But, unfortunately, we also see too clearly the dangers from those fanatics of religion who permit only one vision as the true one, and feel themselves obliged to convert others, and sometimes even condemn or kill those differently committed.

Now we must turn to our own religion, Judaism, and see how this conflict stands with us. In Judaism, we have no single great figure, such as Jesus or Buddha, or a Mohammed or Zarathustra, but a series of comparatively human patriarchs and matriarchs who help us realize that God manifests in history and has a relationship with us, both passionate and particular, both collective and individual. There is, indeed, an image of Israel being married to God.

The great Dutch Protestant theologian, Gerhard van der Leeuw (4), has characterized our spirit not only as a religion of the covenant, but one in which there is unrest—unlike the religions of repose—and this unrest comes from the great Will of God Himself, moving forcefully and compellingly in history, realizing His own aims with us as a partner. Thus, more than with many others, our is a religion of relationship.

Among these patriarchs and matriarchs are the figures of Jacob and his mother, Rebekah. The former, who himself becomes Israel, is a central personality in this history and, as such, is a crucial model for our theme.

The name Jacob means "one who takes by the heel, and thus tries to trip up or supplant" (5, p.354). He is, therefore, a trickster, as his subsequent history shows. He deceives his brother Esau and does the same to his father Isaac, in order to win both the birthright and the blessing. This is hardly an auspicious beginning for a man destined to be the father of all the tribes of Israel! Yet he did this apparently immoral act by dutifully following his mother Rebekah's instruction. And she, in turn, was carefully carrying out what the Lord God Himself had told her. God was apparently going against His own rules. We remember that Rebekah was barren and Isaac entreated the Lord who promptly helped her to conceive. But twins struggled within her womb and she, herself, inquiring of God, was told that two nations struggled in her womb and that the elder would serve the younger. So, when Esau was the first of the twins to be born, followed by Jacob grasping at his heel, she knew that the younger would be her favorite.

We know the story of the subsequent deceptions and of how Jacob, when found out, fled away from his understandably wrathful brother Esau to his uncle's lands where he, himself, was sorely deceived. But even on his way to his uncle Laban, the trickster Jacob was visited by God when he slept at Beth-El, and was told that he would be blessed as the ancestor of a great nation. God would be with him, he was told. And Jacob then witnessed a great ladder ascending into heaven and the angels of God circulating up and down upon it.

So, even this deceiver was chosen by God. We know, furthermore, that after Jacob paid for his own deceptions at the hands of Laban, he went out rich and fruitful, but his own favorite wife, Rachel, suffered barrenness (as did her creative and enterprising predecessor matriarchs, Sarah and Rebekah) and was herself a trickster.

The trickery continued until Jacob made his peace with his uncle and returned, with wives and children and flocks, to the land that God had promised him. Rightfully fearful of his brother Esau's wrath, he sent gifts and also apologized to God, saying "I am not worthy of all the kindness and of all the truth which Thou hast shown unto thy servant" (1, Gen. 32:10).

After this first-time realization or statement of error on his part (can we call it conscience?), Jacob had the memorable night in which he struggled with the angel of God, and held on until he was blessed. At break of day, he was blessed, and called the place Peniel, for he had seen God "face to face" and his life was preserved. After this, Jacob encountered Esau and he "bowed himself to the ground seven times." Esau embraced his brother and they both wept. The subsequent peace and mutual service was a fitting ending to a story which began not only with the birth of the warring brothers but hints back to the conflict between Abel and Cain, and between Isaac and Ishmael. The brothers are reconciled and, finally, Jacob is once more rewarded with an appearance of God who changes his name from Jacob to Israel, from trickster to "Perseveror with God."

This story is central in our connection on several grounds. First, we see a division in the human realm—the theme of the warring brothers and principles—hinting at a division in the divine itself. Did not God reverse his previous pattern of blessing and birthright to the elder son? Did He not abet Rebekah's deception of her husband for His own aims? And why not, since this same God sorely tried his chosen one, Abraham, by ordering him to sacrifice this self-same son, Isaac! We have, here, an image of a God who reverses His own laws, deceives and helps to deceive His favorites, aids the trickster, provides creativity only when importuned, but clearly had method and aim in his plan. The "plain man" and shepherd take precedence over the "hairy man" and hunter. Civilization and cultivation are to carry on the development of society beyond the hunting level of life. And even the idols, carried by Rachel, called "images," are allowed to be brought by her and buried by Jacob. We see in Jacob a powerful description of the struggle within man himself with his own dark side, abetted by the divine. We glimpse the apparent multiplicity of tendencies within the unitary Godhead. It is from this that true conscience is forged.

But what do we mean by conscience? The eminent scholar at Hebrew University in Jerusalem, Zvi Werblowsky, asserts (10, p.81) that "there is no Hebrew equivalent of our Western 'conscience'—not even an approximation." Conscience is derived from the Latin *conscientia*, which means "knowing with" and implies a consciousness which is able to detach itself and enable the person to judge himself. Not so with the Jews, says Werblowsky. For Biblical man, to *be* was to *be addressed* by God. The Lord commanded and man obeyed. Rather, his response was to *hear* the command and obey. Disobedience meant not responding, shutting one's self off from God and from one's true being. The general implication throughout is that God's word is meant to be listened to, from outside of one's self, to effect "the heart" and, ultimately, when the Law is so imbedded on the inner man and "the heart" that they were one.

Werblowsky pursues this theme at length, showing that a deep ethics and morality are not incompatible with a lack of the category of conscience as such, but imply a direct response to God or lack of it. For our purposes, we need only see in deeper measure that in Judaism the theme of struggling with one's conscience is a late development. Our main duty is only to be responsive to God. Once more, relationship is at the center.

How, then, are we to understand the statement by Jacob, quoted earlier, that he was "unworthy" of God's mercy and kindness? Not much had changed in his path of deception. He was just very fearful of Esau's wrath. Or did it change? Can we not speculate that in his anxiety, he turned away from the image of his brother's wrath to that of God Himself? Did not his experience of deception at the hands of Laban teach him something? R. Waddy Moss, scholar of the Hasting's *Dictionary of the Bible* (5, p.454) is of that opinion:

> Alone on the banks of the Jabbok, full of doubt as to the fate that would overtake him, he recognizes at last that his real antagonist is not Esau but God. All his fraud and deceit had been pre-eminently sin against God; and what he needed supremely was not reconciliation with his brother, but the blessing of God.

We can only agree with this perception and add that *Jacob must have recognized that the theft of the "blessing" from his father was as nothing if he did not have the "blessing" of God.* And this was what he sought. He had already "had" it given to him, but now he had to "earn" it, or verify it. Once more, unimpaired relationship, despite previous gifts and promises, is the true "conscience" of the Biblical Jew.

Something similar is implied by the great Jewish scholar, Rabbi Joseph B. Soloveitchik, who, in his moving article, "The Lonely Man of Faith" (6), shows that the man of faith is perforce lonely:

> It is God who wants the man of faith to oscillate between the faith community and the community of majesty, between being confronted by God in the cosmos and the intimate, immediate apprehension of God through the covenant, and who therefore willed that complete human redemption be unattainable.

The religious man, therefore, is not fully at home in any community, and lives the dialectical role assigned to him. Psychologically, we would say that the man of faith, one who has a commitment to the divine principle, perforce lives in a dialectical situation and, therefore, is in struggle. It is from this struggle that what the term conscience is derived, but *it is the Jewish contribution to see that the relationship is primary even though it is the law that is "commanded."*

Whatever it is that we mean by conscience, whether externally derived or inwardly achieved, it is clear that almost everyone has what might be called a "moral reaction." Jung has noted (2) that this is part of nature itself. There is, within the psyche, a propensity to such considerations, even though the actual content of the moral reaction will change from culture to culture, time to time, and, indeed, during the course of an individual's development. The Eskimo, for example, can have a bad conscience when he has skinned an animal with an iron knife instead of the traditional flint one (2, p.188), as well as feel twinges of guilt when he has left a friend in the lurch. In our Jewish tradition, the six-hundred thirteen commandments contain both such laws; the implication is that all of life, every aspect of behavior, is to be sanctified and governed by the law. In this sense is it moral.

Jung points out (2, p.199-200) that:

> Conscience is a psychic reaction which one can call *moral* because it always appears when the conscious mind leaves the path of custom, *mores*, or suddenly recollects it.

It is here that we see that "moral" behavior is linked with patterns and laws. When there is collision among them, or conflict with them, there begins to be the possibility of individual reflection and, therefore, *ethical* behavior can begin. The latter is possible only when there is conscious scrutiny, reflection about two different modes of moral behavior. An individual pattern emerges which can be called ethical rather than strictly moral. This ethic of serving God even against the prevailing moral pattern is apparent in Rebekah.

From a psychological point of view, one can say that such ethical considerations—here defined as requiring reflection and choice, arising out of struggle—produces higher consciousness. This, in turn, promotes new understanding and change in the divine images themselves. Such, I believe, was the experience of Jacob, when he demonstrated his own anxiety upon his return to Esau. He apparently knew that his struggle was with God Himself (when he says that he does not deserve mercy or kindness) but he is surely aware that his very "moral" behavior was invited by God also. His perception gives us a hint of the much later experience of Job, who not only comprehended that God was beyond good and evil, but that a mortal could hold on to his own ethic yet not separate himself from God. This latter realization, I think, became possible as a profound development from what Jacob experienced, leading to a continuing change in our own images of the divine.

Jacob was given "the truth," face to face, he tells us, and Job saw the back of God. So seeing, he put his hand over his mouth, he silenced himself. They both had deepened understanding of the nature of the divine image itself.

Jung has contributed an affecting discussion of the development of religious consciousness in his book, *Answer to Job.* In our present connection, I want only to point out that it is in this kind of conflict, in which psychic struggle occurs, including both collective patterns or *mores* and individual reflections, that consciousness grows. Tradition and autonomy collide in the soul of the individual and produce a truly *psychological* conscience that we can term ethics. By this we mean that the person has a hard-won personal standpoint, arising out of the struggle between what is "given" and what his own nature demands, and, at last, turns to his own images of the divine for a resolution. In this, his ethics become individual.

If we turn, now, to how these considerations appear in psychotherapeutic practice, in the rough-and-tumble of the struggle between autonomy and tradition, individual and collective, as it occurs in the painful reflections of people undergoing analysis, we are surprised.

The struggle between individual and collective, or, for example, between morality and desire, becomes manifest only when the person experiences guilt. And this guilt is by no means connected with religious considerations among most people who enter psychotherapy. Rather, we see that the psyches of most beginners on the psychological path of development are filled with all sorts of images and qualities which belong to past or historical religious attitudes but are not experienced as such by the person. How many drug addicts or alcoholics, for example, realize that they are failed Dionysians, that they are in the grip of a god known well by the Greeks but that they neither honor it nor struggle with it? How many atheists carry around within themselves a harsh and critical inner judge who condemns every deviation, however slight, from an attitude of rationalism and materialism? And how many pleasure-seekers are filled with the pagan lusts of Pan or the self-adornment of Aphrodite, without the religious attitude that the Greeks had, which made these experiences profound, blissful and in the service of culture?

In short, we find that the images and beliefs of old are carried around in the psyches of modern men, just as Rachel carried her old "images" when she accompanied Jacob. These, too, are "buried," just as Jacob did, but now in the unconscious and they emerge in people's dreams and fantasies as multiple tendencies toward experience and behavior. As people become aware of this inner diversity and potency, they learn that the demonization of parent and culture, of friend and foe, is a projection of their own inner "gods," named more banally as archetypes in our psychological jargon, and that their outer attitude of atheism or agnosticism, or even of belief in a particular religion, belies the true character of their own psyches.

In the work of therapy, people discover their own dark side, their shadows, as Jung called it, but also, in time, they also discover the collective shadows and images that belong to us all. To continue with the process is to become more conscious and to take on the problem of uniting consciousness with the unconscious, and to both create and discover one's own ethic or ways of being. In so doing, the individual becomes like Jacob himself, struggling with the angels—and demons—which present themselves in his/her psyche. One seeks a blessing, a harmony with the divine or higher authority as it is discovered within one's self. The price we pay for this consciousness—and relationship—as with Jacob, is a deep wound. We are marked in the sinews. Jacob's way—as is the way of all the founding patriarchs and matriarchs—is that of individuation writ large, the collective individuation of an entire culture.

On our ordinary human level, such conflict is less heroic and more banal—fraught with daily frustration, the requirements of survival, and not so grand. The conscience that people discover—particularly if they are not in loving connection with a religious tradition—is usually harsh, mechanical and quite uninspired. The inner voice is simply uncaring, treats the person like a machine, or is equally condemning of others who do not do as the person wishes or this voice righteously demands. And, strangely, people succumb to this voice, not by obeying its commands, usually, but by often going against it, but then suffering its endless abuse. Surprisingly—if one considers the Freudian conception of the superego, for example—such a harshness was not generally experienced by the person in his own childhood. Rather, it seems that this collectively experienced moralizer is just the result of an image of "god," as one might call it, *who no longer has a true relationship to the ego.* It is a part soul gone bad. And patients usually find remarkable the suggestion that one could answer back to this inner voice and say to it, for example, "I am no mere machine. Why do you treat me so badly and without human regard?" It is as difficult to say "No" to such a tyrannical god as it is to say "No" to the other tyrannical gods of desire!

It is possible, however, to engage in a relationship with these diverse inner strivings and promptings and to acknowledge that one's psyche is the home for them, and the ego is an agent, or mediator, trying to reconcile these as best he/she can. When one takes on such a struggle—"struggling with the old images of god fallen into the unconscious" one might say—the outcome is true autonomy and individuality, which both honors tradition and the self. This, at deeper levels, is experienced as a religious struggle, and one's images of the divine itself perforce change. I think, now, of a committed Hindu who, in the course of his analysis, re-discovered the rejected Christian aspects of himself, to say nothing of the pagan, and the process was one of discovering/creating a most individual religious attitude. I think, too, of several young Jews who had immersed themselves in various eastern religions and sects and finally had to come home to their own Jewishness. Not as the prodigal son, I hasten to add, since their apostasy and embrace of the alien was just as real as their return or *teshuva*, but they, too, had to find an individual way to the God that was discovered both in their own souls and revealed in the tradition into which they were born.

The foregoing examples sound a bit grand, I know, but they are, indeed, no whit different from the more frequent, ordinary and banal struggle that we all have with these archetypes within ourselves, whether interpreted as "remnants" or "vestiges" or experienced with the full power of the numinous. Some people can find their reconciliation within themselves without the long, hazardous path of the inner night-sea journey. Others need to find and live their own myth, their own story of relationship to the divine. For those who can do this and remain within the sacred dimension of tradition, such as is described by Rabbi Soloveitchik, all the better. For those who can not, they can comfort themselves with the possibility that the divine is working in them, too, and that it seeks a particular realization and fulfillment which is vouchsafed no one else in that unique way. In this struggle, whether within tradition or outside of it, we all succeed and we all fail, since we are always dealing with the *images* of the divine which are manifested in us, and we know, as is revealed in Kabbalah, that the *Ain Soph*, the God which lies beyond and transcends all images, is the One we finally serve. As with Jacob's vision of the circulating angels on the ladder to heaven, we work from manifestation to transcendence and the reverse. In this struggle, we honor what is revealed, what finds its home in our psyches. We are true inheritors of the Covenant, thereby, since we serve a never-ending relationship with God as is discovered in tradition, in experience and in one's self.

As I was thinking of a clinical example of such a struggle between tradition and autonomy, with the resultant change in the image of God, what came to me was an incident in my own experience. Permit my clinical example to be myself. In 1966, a friend and I had a serious falling out with senior colleagues over our being elevated to the post of training analyst. Our belief was that our judges were unjust and unable to dialogue with us. They had equally negative opinions of us. One day, after a totally unfruitful attempt to dialogue with them, I realized that, in conscience, I had to resign from my loved and respected community of Jungians, since I could neither submit to their judgment, nor convince them. Conscience led to aloneness.

As I drove home over the hill, weeping profusely over this loss and with my pain, I had a vision of two old men, grandfathers who came to me after the break with my spiritual fathers. One of these two was my actual grandfather, an orthodox Jew who died at the age of 97. I visited him weekly during the first year of my analysis, back in 1950, the last one of his life. For me he represented all that was enduring and whole in our Jewish tradition. The second grandfather was C.G. Jung, whose work had absorbed me from the age of twenty-four onwards and who is, in my view, the leading spiritual figure of the twentieth century. These two, one a symbol of tradition, the other a symbol of individuation, came to me and embraced me. They laughed and drew me to them, and we all danced a *hora*. With this vision, I was able to go on, to project less on temporary collectives—such as societies—for my spiritual community, and to stand alone. It took me fourteen years, just like Jacob, to once again resume my membership in that society, and be less demanding of it.

More importantly, it took all those years for me to solidify my own uniqueness, and to creatively relate to a larger world that was represented to me in those earlier days. Like Jacob, I had to struggle with my own images of God, until I understood more "truth" and could also come to a place where I, too, could "bow seven times." In all those years, my own struggle was with the image of God, as revealed to me from inner depths, and I wrote several books mirroring that struggle. (7,8,9).

So, I am deeply indebted to the figure of Jacob in our tradition, which, incidentally, was also the name of my grandfather and is one Hebrew name of my son, as well. For the pursuit of individuation, I am also indebted most profoundly to C.G. Jung, who wrote as follows (3, p.452):

> Individuation and collectivity are a pair of opposites, two divergent destinies. They are related to one another by guilt. The individual is obliged by the collective demands to purchase his individuation at the cost of an equivalent work for the benefit of society. So far as this is possible, individuation is possible.

Finally, I need to remind myself of the acclamation of the *Shema* in our faith: we proclaim our commitment to God as One. Psychologically, in addition, we know that the One is "given" as a beginning, but also is a consequence of deep inner work. This Oneness, furthermore, surely makes possible a unity between tradition and autonomy, *boruch hashem.*

REFERENCES

1. The Bible, Masoretic text in English, Jewish Publication Society of America, 1917. (King James version has "mercy" in place of "kindness.")

2. Jung, C.G. "A Psychological View of Conscience," in *Conscience*, Various Hands, edited by Curatorium of the C.G. Jung Institute Zurich, Northwestern University Press, Evanston, 1970, pp. 181-201.

3. Jung, C.G. *The Symbolic Life.*, Collected Works, Vol. 18.

4. Leeuw, Gerhard van der, *Religion in Essence and Manifestation,*. George Allen and Unwin, London, 1938, 709 pp. (original 1933)

5. Moss, R. Waddy. "Jacob," in *Hasting's Dictionary of the Bible*, Charles Scribner's Sons, New York, 1963, pp. 453-455.

6. Soloveitchik, Rabbi, "The Lonely Man of Faith," *Tradition*, Vol. 7, No. 2, 1965.

7. Spiegelman, J. Marvin, *The Tree: Tales in Psychomythology*, Falcon Press, Phoenix, 1982. 464 pp. (original 1974)

8. Spiegelman, J. Marvin, *The Quest,* Falcon Press, Phoenix, 1984, 175 pp.

9. Spiegelman, J. Marvin, *Jungian Psychology and the Passions of the Soul,* Falcon Press, Las Vegas, 1989. 446 + ix pp.

10. Werblowsky, R.J. Zwi, "The Concept of Conscience in Jewish Perspective," in *Conscience*, Various Hands, edited by the Curatorium, C.G. Jung Institute, Zurich, Northwestern University Press, Evanston, 1970, pp. 81-109.

JUDAISM AND JUNGIAN PSYCHOLOGY:
A PERSONAL EXPERIENCE

(From *A Modern Jew in Search of a Soul*, ed. Spiegelman and Jacobson)

The following is a case-study of "A Modern Jew in Search of a Soul." The case is that of myself, although I shall be summoning up experiences of others and making generalizations which may have a larger application. How can I dare do this? How can one be so foolhardy or self-centered as to use his own experiences particularly those of an inner life, to describe such a collective condition as the contemporary Jew coming to terms with his Jewishness and himself ? In a typically Jewish fashion, I shall answer that question with a question: How else can one do it? Are we not all encased within our own psyches, bounded not only by an impinging environment, but also by the heredity which we bring to life? Our individuality, both potential and actualized, results from an interaction between the "given" and the "possible," as my favorite Dutch Protestant theologian Gerhard van der Leeuw put it (1).We are born into or "given" time, place, family, tribe, etc., but we are also free to develop, to change, to combine, those "givens" in new possibilities or wholes. In short, I am presenting my personal myth, as Jung called it.

Another piece of my personal myth (not the Jewish part) was included in a book written by my friend and colleague, Mokusen Miyuki, and myself, called *Buddhism and Jungian Psychology* (2). Toward the end of writing that book, I was visited by a bad conscience: Why was I not writing about Jungian psychology and my own tradition, Judaism? As I sweated this question and was resolving to do such a work, my publisher at Falcon Press asked me to participate in this present book,*[A Modern Jew in Search of a Soul]*. The synchronicity seemed meaningful and precise: I should continue with this explication of my personal myth, since the network of lines of fate, the force field of events, was welcoming it. So here it is.

What is that strange myth that has a Jew writing about himself in the context of Jungian Psychology and Buddhism, and then Judaism and Jungian Psychology? Is he a Japanese Jew? No, not quite. But, in the second year of his analysis, at the age of twenty-five, he had a big dream and vision at Christmas time in which he witnessed the birth of a divine child—not an already born one, such as Jesus—but a new one. Three new "kings" or wise men were there to welcome the birth of this child and to nourish its development. These kings were a Jewish rabbi, a Christian priest, and a Buddhist priest. So, then, in a not atypical Jungian fashion, part of my myth has been ecumenical. In order to develop that representation of divine wholeness in my Self, I have needed to pursue deeply both a Christian and a Buddhist strand in my soul, as well as my basic Jewish core.

This ecumenical myth, as a matter of fact, is not so strange after all. I have met more than one person, of different religious and ethnic background, who has been similarly propelled. I reported a dream of such a person, which foresaw a religious structure of the future incorporating all of the triad of my own myth plus others, in my paper on "Psychotherapy and the Clergy: Fifty Years later" (3). All of us, furthermore, who have read Jung's *Memoirs*, (4) remember his profound experience in his seventies, when he dreamed ecumenically on three successive nights. He experienced the exaltation of the Jewish image of Kabbalistic union of Malkuth with Tifereth, the Christian Marriage of the Lamb, and the pagan Greek *hierosgamos* (p. 294). Indeed, I think that my myth, like Jung's, is an individuation story.

This ecumenical myth, with its historical roots, seems to be afoot generally. Many of us need to not only find and buttress our uniqueness, but also to link ourselves with the rest of humankind. Only in such a way can we build that more complete future for which we long. Even as I formulate this longing, I hear the Jewish voice speaking, the echo of the religious prophets of the past, of Moses and Isaiah, and of even that benighted and anti-Semitic Jewish prophet of the last century, Karl Marx, who also longed for a future paradise, an anti-utopian utopia, in which heaven comes to earth and we are redeemed in community (5). Jung, too, I think, is part of this prophetic tradition, and we even draw our very title from him, *Modern Man in Search of a Soul*. (6). The conclusion he draws, of the need to strengthen the individual against atomization and collectivization, is one strand in the dilemma of individuality and community.

I return, now, to my personal story. I was born into the Jewish community of East Los Angeles in 1926 to a mother who immigrated from England as an infant and a father who came from Poland in his late teens. All my grandparents were from Poland, city and village, forest and *shtefl*. My parents were social democrats, America-loving and eager to move away from the poverty and religious rigidity of their origins. My paternal grandparents, who arrived in the United States only shortly before I was born, when my grandfather was already seventy, belonged to the past—they were wholly orthodox, religious, and closer to the Middle Ages than the Twentieth century. My grandfather, particularly, seemed like Moses to me, with his white beard, deep blue eyes, imposing patriarchal manner, husband of two women (sequentially) and father of many children. He was an important figure to me, about which I shall have much to say presently.

The general theme of this family, however, like so many others, was the maintenance of family ties, of kinship, of survival and advancement beyond poverty, of social justice and service. The strands of Americanization, socialist ideology, hope for Israel, etc. were much like those of other Jewish families who immigrated from Eastern Europe to find new life in the Promised Land of America. They often tended to lose their deeply religious and community oriented philosophy, and to embrace new images of redemption. I have used this kind of material, fictionalized, in my story of Julia, the Atheist-Communist, in my book, *The Tree: Tales* in *Psychomythology* (7). I shall refer more fully to these stories later on, but here, suffice it to say that the image of *Haskala,* of the Jews of the *shtetl* and the enclosed community of the faithful leaving it and joining the world, was the theme therein. The world was discovered but God got lost.

Not so for my grandfather, I hasten to add, who provided a physical link with tradition for me and, in the years of my first analysis, served as a symbol for that link spiritually.

The Jewish content of my life as a child was not particularly profound nor complete. There was the gastronomic Jewishness of traditional Friday night dinners and Sunday breakfasts of bagels, cream cheese and lox. There was the observance of certain festivals at my grandparent's house: Passover, the High Holidays. In that sense, there was a celebration of kinship and community, but of religious content, only a little. What I did recall of the divine element, was visiting my grandfather in temple during the High Holidays. The old men would gather in the basement of the synagogue during the day and there was serious *davenning*. In the swaying and intensity of the old men, their religious fervor was apparent. They were different from the members of the upper gallery for whom fine clothes and appearance carried more weight. I suspect that many of my generation will recognize some of their own experience in what I describe here.

But there was Jewish education as well for me and my fellow young males, but not much for the females. We went to Hebrew school for several years, but of the socialist Workmen's Circle type. We studied Yiddish, reading and writing, but not enough Hebrew to really use it, and little of the Bible. These thrice-weekly after-school sessions, however, were often missed, fought against and derided by my young ruffian friends and myself. Better to play handball against the garages nearby than attend the boring classes. Poor Mr. Perlmutter, our teacher, and how unkind we were to him! Jews with no soul might have been his judgment of us, indeed, and with right. All that changed when we were in "basic training" at synagogue for the bar mitzvah, however. Now there were serious things to learn: the prayers, the commentaries, the particular portion to be read, the speech to be written and memorized. Now, perhaps, the religious-sense began playing a role. We had to submit to discipline, to an "initiation into adulthood" (at thirteen?—our ancestors were more mature, to be sure). There began to be some link between the private experiences of God that I had as a child and these events, but the connection was vague and not a source of significant conflict or importance. There was such a thing as being Jewish, important as much for the minority aspect as anything else, but this was different from those experiences of the soul which a later self would describe as numinous, as tinged with awe and wonder. Jewish life was social life, except for *Zaideh,* my grandfather, who carried both.

I would say, then, that my Jewish religious life was essentially lacking until I began my own analysis at the age of twenty-four with a German-Jewish survivor of the concentration camps, Dr. Max Zeller. Here was an educated, cultured man who was also religious! This was rare among the teachers and professors I had known.

Besides this incongruity, I had the shock of my life within a few months of beginning my analytic work. I had completed my first Active Imagination, a work with fantasy in which the person continues a kind of dialogue with dream figures. This active fantasy included some water-color paintings and a description of a relationship with an unknown female dancer. It was called "Purple in the Blue." I brought it to my analytic session and, in the waiting room, I happened to look at some books of the *Zohar* (8), which had just arrived. Opening one of the volumes at random, I read material which was very much like what I had written in my own fantasy! Tremblingly, I went upstairs to report this event to my analyst and was so struck by this synchronicity that it took me sixteen years to really look at these books again. I had to study all sorts of other mysticism and religious experience before I had the courage to return. Only later did I discover that it was also part of that same Jewish mystical tradition that one should not undertake Kabbalistic study until the age of forty. So, l was a proper Jewish pupil after all! As a "A Modern Jew in Search of a Soul," I had found within myself an undeniable and uncanny link with my Jewish heritage that was to permanently change my direction. At the same time, I had dreams about my grandfather and felt a longing to speak with him more fully about the family, the past, and Jewish matters. I therefore supplemented my analytic sessions with frequent visits to my grandparents, where I was cordially received. This was in 1951, the last year of his life, when he was in his ninety-seventh year. My grandmother, too, surely fulfilled for me the archetypal Great Mother with her kindness, humor and goodwill. She, also, lived into her nineties.

Even now, as I write, I recall those visits with emotion. And I also recall the equally profound event of an earlier time, when I was eighteen, in the Merchant Marine, and about to go on a war-time voyage around the world. My grandfather, when he saw me in my cadet-midshipman's uniform, gave me a blessing. It was a blessing, of course, for a safe-journey, but it was also, as I later learned and experienced, a blessing in the ancient sense, like that of Jacob by his father Isaac. I was deeply moved by this event, and felt it most profoundly. I knew that I had to continue the family spirit in some way, and carry on that which my grandfather had valued so highly. I, too, like the Biblical Jacob, was not the oldest grandchild, but felt singled out. This was in harmony with my religious experience as a very young child in which I felt a specialness of connection with the God above (associated with the sun). So, now, my Jewish vocation was anchored, not only by the blessing of my grandfather, but by the psychic events of my early analysis. A modern Jew was in search of his soul, indeed!

There was no more particularly Jewish content in my analytic work for the next two or so years, although there were themes, such as the flood, which hearkened back to Biblical events. I also profited very much from attending seminars on a Jungian view of certain Biblical tales, provided, for example, by the visiting Swiss-Jewish Jungian Analyst, Rivkah Schaerf-Kluger (9). She also gave a deeply affecting seminar on the as-yet-untranslated book of Jung, *Answer to Job* (10). That book was to have a great influence upon me and is, I think, one of his most important contributions, particularly to Jews and to those of us who are both deeply committed to our origins and alive to the changes the soul is undergoing. I shall have more to say about this later on. At present, however, I wish to return to the final strikingly Jewish event to occur during my first analysis. Once more this involves my grandfather, although he had died two years earlier.

It was the fall of 1953. I was about to complete my analysis, and was facing a call-up into military service within a few months. It was during the Korean War, in which I was to serve for two years as an Army Psychologist. Also, I was about to get married. One night, thinking about these things, and also wondering what to do in the way of ritual for my forthcoming marriage, I went to the La Brea Tar Pits park, a place that I had frequented when I lived in that area from ages ten to eighteen. In 1953, it was still an oasis of solitude in the midst of the surrounding city, and I sat upon a bench in quiet reflection. All at once, I felt my grandfather present, not as a ghost, but as a quality of personality. Without words, he suggested/ordered me to stand up and walk. Without cavil, I did so, and began to walk up Fairfax boulevard, towards the Jewish community district. After a few blocks, my grandfather directed me to cross the street and go into a building. It was not until I was close to the building that I recognized it as a synagogue. Opening the door—it was a Friday night—I saw ahead of me, praying and speaking to an assembled congregation, a man who looked remarkably like my grandfather. He was tall, white bearded, strong-faced, and he *davened* with great intensity.

I knew at once that this was the rabbi that my grandfather wanted to conduct the marriage ceremony. After the service, I went up to him and learned that he was named Rabbi Jacob (like my grandfather!) Sonderling.

He said that he would be happy to perform the ceremony for us, but would like to meet with us first. I was delighted and, when we chatted a little, was surprised to discover that he had a Ph.D. (just as I had received the year before), but in philosophy, not psychology. He studied the psychology of aesthetics, however, and had been a pupil of Ebbinghaus, no less. This seemed synchronistic, to be sure, and I thanked my grandfather, inwardly, for directing me to such a fine and kind gentleman. The synchronicity did not end at that point, however.

When my bride-to-be met with Rabbi Sonderling, it emerged that he had known her paternal grandfather in Europe during World War I. Rabbi Sonderling was a rabbi in the Germany army, at the time, and was touring the border areas of Poland on behalf of the German Jewish community, to assist the *shtetls* with what they might need. Rabbi Sonderling was particularly impressed by my wife's grandfather, Rabbi Silberstein, in that he asked only that his community continue to be able to honor the Sabbath totally, rather than serve German soldiers on that day. Piety over profit, even for impoverished Jews, was an impressive value. This link, then, with the grandfathers of my wife and myself was very moving for us. The wedding ceremony was one that we will never forget. The power of it made it clear to me that whatever one's inner religious experience, it is essential that certain collective events always belong with the community, and that the psyche itself longs for this. As I was also to realize later on with the births of my children, all these turning-point events required collective celebration and ritual. I would say, therefore, that birth, initiation, marriage and death are the minimum four passages to be so fulfilled. It is in this sense that I agree with one derivation of the word *religio* as "linking back." It is a linking with God in community and tradition.

How, then, is one to understand these powerfully Jewish impressions from my early analysis and at its conclusion? Why did it happen this way and what was my psyche trying to communicate to me? I think that these psychological events were "timed," as it were. Whenever there is a con-catenation of an inner condition and an outer meaningful event, as Jung termed synchronicity, strong emotions are present. When, in addition, these synchronistic events, with their archetypal connection, also touch upon collective rituals, celebrations and "sacred time," as Eliade calls it (11), an especially large quantum of psychic energy is released. It has been at particular conjunctions of outer sacred events and inner work that such potent and meaningful experiences have occurred. This has been especially noteworthy for me with Jewish events, but they have also occurred at moments sacred to Christian and Buddhist tradition. For example, my fundamental myth experience of the three kings or priests took place precisely at Christmas time; and my experience of speaking in Tokyo on East and West occurred not only at the time of Buddha's birthday, but along with me on the podium were both Buddhist and Christian priests!

This, then, is one link between the ongoing psychological or inner experience of a religious nature, so fully described by Jung, and that of community tradition. Jung has preferred the derivation of *religio* as "careful observation of the numinous," which associates it more with individual experience. My inner or psychologically observed religious experiences have been quite frequent, if not ongoing, although their link with community has been relatively rare, but profound. I believe, then, that my psyche was providing itself both a base and an outer connection during this first experience of my analytic youth, so to speak, and this was necessary to support the requirement of standing alone, of which Jung speaks. In short, I really needed to know who I was, both personally and collectively, before I could truly embrace my utter particularity later in life.

Such a necessity to stand alone did occur later in life, when I was forty, and that, too involved the image of my grandfather. One spring afternoon, after a totally frustrating experience of injustice on the part of senior Jungian colleagues, I decided to resign my membership in the local society. As I drove home in tears, I experienced deeply what felt like utter betrayal at the hands of my analytic fathers. This was in marked contrast to my own father, who had always been a source of warmth and emotional support. As I crossed the mountain pass on the way to my home, I had a vision of my grandfather, once more, and Jung, both of whom came forward to embrace me. There was love and joy in their faces as they pulled me to them. At the next moment, the three of us were dancing a *hora* which felt like the ecstatic celebrations of the *Hasidim*. I knew, then, that I was connected, inwardly, to my Jewish heritage, as represented by my grandfather, and to the spirit of my own individuation as represented by Jung. Yet there was an inner similarity between Jung and my grandfather. When I completed my studies in Switzerland, I felt the need to see Jung alone and to receive his blessing in some way as a prelude to doing analytic work. I had passed the requirements, but the image of the blessing was strong for me, just as it had been when my grandfather blessed me when I went off to war. Jung obliged me, in our session, which I have described elsewhere (12). Suffice to say here that he, too, gave me a link with God, by his being, by his manner of relating and by example.

Since that time of the "hora" with Jung and my grandfather, the latter's image has no longer appeared as such, but there have been variants of the archetype behind my experience of him in much of my fictional writing. Indeed, it was only after that separation/individuation from my local society that my particular brand of fictional writing, psycho-mythology, began.

From that time onwards, my Jewish experiences—of an inner nature, at least—have lost much of their particularity and have blended in with the totality of my myth. For example, in *The Tree* (13), there are three specifically Jewish story-tellers out of ten. That is a "minyan" of five men and five women, each of whom represents a different religion, belief system or attitude, but all carrying out their-own individuation. Of the three Jews included, one is a Knight (14). His story, of the fragmentation of the divine and the need of God for humanity in order to be whole, is connected with Jewish gnosticism. A second Jew is Julia, the Atheist-Communist, whom I mentioned before, and a third is the Medium, Sophie-Sarah. The latter examines the Holocaust from a Kabbalistic point-of-view. Jewish elements appear in other parts of the ten tales, as they also do in the sequels to the first book, *The Quest* (15) and *The Love* (16). These, as I say, are blended, so that in the inner realm, at least, they constitute parts of the totality.

Inner blending did not result in an integrated connection to religious community, however. An understanding of this failure was made clearer to me from a dream I had at the time of my son's bar-mitzvah. Several years before this event, our family joined an orthodox synagogue and I participated in this process of my son's education by going to Saturday services with him and by having frequent discussions with the rabbi. I even spent some time examining a Jewish mystical text together with him. The night before the day of my son's ritual initiation, however, and in the full flush of excitement and preparation, I dreamed as follows:

> I am in a room adjacent to the synagogue. It is like the study room in which I had the discussions with the rabbi, but also has the quality of the sacristy in Catholic churches, where the priest dresses for the service. In this room, I am at first looking through drawers, trying to find a white dress shirt which fits me. Preparations are going on next door for the bar-mitzvah and the regular Saturday service and I am afraid I we will be late. I search for a shirt, but they are all too small. I notice that some of them belong to the father of my son's friend, a man who is in no way psychological and is quite content to be a member of the congregation. But his shirts don't fit me. I start to get a bit frantic, especially when I notice that there is also present a German-Jewish acquaintance who is a woman particularly finicky about doing things according to the rules. Her disapproval of my clothes also bothers me. I shrug my shoulders, however, and gesture to her my incapacity to find the right shirt and my apology therefore. At that moment she vanishes, and I am, instead, with the rabbi. We look at each other deeply, but silently. There is an appreciation of each other, but a recognition of our differences also. We then look up at the ceiling of the room, which has a silk covering. This silk is very beautiful, but there is a large rent in it. As the rabbi and I look at this torn silk covering, we nod, as if we understand that the "fabric," meaning the fabric of Jewish wholeness, is torn. He and I are together, however, and my son, next door, will be undergoing his bar-mitzvah alone, but with God. As the dream ends, I hear my son

chanting with great feeling and joy as he concludes the prayers. I am relieved that he can do it for himself.

The dream, I think, requires no interpretation, but only comment. In point of fact, it was and is difficult for me to be a member of a congregation: I don't have the right *persona* for it, in Jung's sense, or the social know-how. I always am moved and deepened by the services, but find the institutional obligations onerous. Nor can I satisfy the requirements of fitting in with the proper rules. That is certainly my own inadequacy. The dream says, however, that there is also a rent in the fabric of Jewish existence. Ever since the destruction of the Temple, that tornness is felt in the endless persecutions in the Diaspora and the present division in Jewish life (as in my stories) among the orthodoxly observant, the "Protestant reformation" (Conservative, Reform, and Reconstructionist Judaism), and the "socialist," "individualist" or "humanist" Jews who embrace *Haskala*. There are people, like myself, furthermore, who are deeply religious inwardly, but who can belong to none of these sects of the larger Jewish community—or any other for that matter—but feel akin to all of them. Our condition is like the Modern Man that Jung referred to. He was speaking of the European who was both Protestant and Catholic and could easily see the values and limitations of each. He had hope for the European of the future, therefore, who was inwardly both. Jung himself, however, was something other as well. I have already referred to the great dream of his seventies, in which he experienced the heights of the three divine Jewish, Christian and pagan Greek images. Do I delude myself by averring that my own experiences also move in this direction? Obviously, I think not. And I would add that there is no doubt whatsoever that my deep commitment in this life is to my Jewish "given" and I still work on finding a way to connect that inner multiplicity to some outer Jewish vessel, which this book also symbolizes.

For many years that vessel has been provided by a familial celebration of holidays at our own "temple," our home. This, of course, is itself a deeply Jewish tenet: the home and family, not synagogue, is at the center of Jewish observance. In the last few years, however, I have also been attending High Holiday services under the leadership of my friend and former pupil, Rabbi Levi Meier, who is also a contributor to this book. The gift to my soul, that my family and friends can attend these services, and that my son plays the *shofar,* is an indication that it is possible to unite inner and outer, at least at times. In the synchronicity of time, even this book—to which several Jews of different stripe contribute—indicates this possibility of a congregation of the spirit. All of us have experienced the rending, the endurance of which may be necessary until our wholeness is born from the struggle.

That now brings me to some transpersonal considerations. I belong to that group of "individual" Jews, who constitute one branch of the modern Jewish condition. Others, as in my stories, are the socialist/social democrats, the religiously observant, the ethnic Jews of various stripes, among others. Indeed, one can say that of the Jews who have survived the Holocaust and world persecution, there are still "three opinions for each two Jews," yet all of them can find a psychological space in the modern state of Israel. Even those extreme religious Jews who reject statehood until the coming of the Messiah can find a home there. Indeed, the modern symbol for Jewish life and existence is Israel itself. It is the one communality which is defended by almost all of us and looked upon with great emotion. Some have even said that Israel has taken the place of God for the contemporary Jew! As a symbol, that may be true, although one would have to add that the state is a manifestation of the earthing of the ancient image of return.

From a psychological point-of-view, I want to mention just three themes which I find are central in the spiritual dimension of Jewish life. The first of these is the question of the clash of certain opposites, such as individual vs. community, full Torah observance vs. flexibility. A spokesperson of the Halachic way of life is to be found in the inspired writing of Rabbi Joseph Soloveitchik, whose *Halachic Man* (17) and *Lonely Man of Faith* (18) are marvels of the expression of the traditional way of life, enlivened by clarity of vision and eloquence of faith. A person reading such work wants to immediately wear phylacteries and live an observant life. From him one can realize that all life is sacred and that the living of the mitzvoth is an ideal way to manifest the divine in everyday human existence.

Yet there is a rent in Jewish existence and it will continue—as the ultra—orthodox agree—until the Messiah comes. From a psychological point-of-view that redemption can also appear inwardly, with the individual. It does show itself sometimes with those of us who work deeply with souls of seekers. That separation also shows itself, outwardly and inwardly, I believe, by the changing attitude towards the feminine and women in modern life generally. There is no doubt that the Crown of Kabbalah must unite with his feminine counterpart, Shekinah, here in life, that God must be whole in a masculine and feminine way. This union needs to appear both in the soul and in community. The issue begins to be joined by some women, such as Greenberg (19), and there is representation of such seeking in the present volume. My own view is that the Kabbalistic tradition of Jewish mysticism, as a counter-pole to the *Halachic* observance of Rabbi Soloveitchik, provides a key.

Yet much of what changes in Jewish life and belief will be wrought as a result of the women's movement and must come from women themselves. As I write these words, I come into possession of a dream from a modern Jewish woman, who has had little religious education, but in middle life finds a need for an outer realization and connection with inner experiences. She dreams as follows:

> I am in the newly rebuilt synagogue at B Temple. It is simple and clean, white and airy, with raised ceiling and small balcony. I must be sitting near the front. To my amazement congregants are rising one by one and each person is describing the wound of his early childhood. Each statement is precise and clear using Kleinian, Jungian and Freudian vernacular. People rise and speak from all over the Temple. I am awe struck. The consciousness I have been searching for is here in this newly constructed Temple. Is my function as witness or are these voices aspects of me? I do not see myself speak yet. Maybe the Rabbi is present.

As with my own dream, I will here comment rather than interpret. This rebuilt Temple does not yet exist. In our dreamer's case, there is a combination of a psychological attitude and a religious one. Notably, the sects in the depth psychological tradition are now able to be unified within a religious vessel, and each individual carries weight and importance. At long last, the Temple becomes a true place for the soul and community. But the dreamer, a woman both modern and conscious, does not yet speak. The voice of women, of the feminine, is not yet fully heard. This dream, like my own, is ecumenical yet individual, religious and psychological, but both the new voice and the manifestation of the collective experience in the world is not yet ready. We can only be patient until this newer unity makes itself felt.

The third theme I wish to mention is that of the sundering not only within the Jewish soul, but in the cleavage which exists between it and the daughter religions of Christianity and Islam, and between these and the other great religions of the world, particularly in the Orient. Not long ago, in Jerusalem, I heard a lecture by Professor Zwi Werblowsky of Hebrew University, who began his comments by saying that he was going to speak about the "three great world religions." He paused at this meeting of analysts reverencing a day of sharing among Christians and Muslims and Jews, and went on to say that the these great world religions were Hinduism, Buddhism and Taoism!

The more painful rift to be examined first, I believe, is the specter of growing assimilation on the part of Jews in the Diaspora. The threat to Jewish communities everywhere is compensated by the strength and vigor of Israel. From a psychological point of view, however, the issue is not only social and lack of Jewish education. As an analyst, I have seen Jewish patients who have needed very much to come to terms with Christian imagery and symbols, sometimes even coming close to being assimilated, in the sense of conversion. Usually this work leads to a deeper sense of appreciation of the "other" and the capacity to relate to it. Indeed, I think that the very psychological work done to grasp this "other" is what permits one to come to the deeper truths of one's self. I am more of a Jew myself, for example, for having had the necessity of connecting more deeply with the Christianity in my own soul. A great help in this inner and outer relationship to the attractive and oppressive "other" of Christianity, I believe, is the work of C.G. Jung. His book, *Answer to Job* (20), in particular, provides an astonishing psychological history of the development of consciousness of the divine in our western tradition. It is the only work I know of that really can be said to be true to a "Judeo Christian" continuity. Usually that word tastes bad in the mouth and is said as if one is combining an oriental martial art with Christianity. In Jung's case, however, every Jew can feel his confrontation with the image of God given to us. The resulting experience, of the wholeness of God, light and dark, masculine and feminine, which Jung's work leads to, is closer to our Jewish tradition than most of what Christian understanding has offered thus far.

In many ways, Jung approaches the Kabbalistic conception, but, apparently, it was only later that he learned fully what Jewish mysticism was about. In any case, I believe that this inner and outer confrontation with our daughter-sister religion is what is needed, particularly since we rightly demand that a western, Christian civilization become conscious of the damage that it has done to our people and soul. Certainly there are those in that community who are doing so. How many of us Jews, however, are prepared to take on an inner dialogue with the heretical God-Man? My own attempts (21), are satisfying to me, as are my continuing intimate relationships with committed Christians—and Buddhists—both in individual friendships and in a several-years-old-experiment called the "Psycho-Ecumenical Group." This gathering of people includes those who are simultaneously psychotherapists and members of the clergy: an orthodox rabbi, a Catholic priest, two nuns, an Episcopal priest, a Protestant minister, as well as a Buddhist priest and a layman (myself). We are well aware of these issues, and our continuing meeting makes me hopeful of the future for us all.

The three themes I have mentioned are capable of further emendation, but I want to close this presentation with a final dream, this time not my own but my father's. He, and many of his generation, did not consciously feel strongly about religion at all, and he still does not do so. Now, in his eighty-fifth year, *boruch ha-shem,* he still enjoys a zestful life and appreciation of an ethnic Judaism alone. Yet he dreamed some years ago, when he suffered a most rare incidence of illness, as follows. He finds himself in the forests of his Polish boyhood, and is deeply affected by the intense green and the beauty. Then he is somewhere else in Europe and it is after the Holocaust. Everywhere he looks there is only destruction. Only small stones and bits of broken human objects are visible—a complete rubble. Then he sees only one thing that is undamaged: it is a stand upon which the Torah normally rests on the *bimah*. At that moment, he hears and then sees great numbers of youth, who are now coming to re-build once more. End of dream.

Such a dream from a Jew who does not acknowledge religious sentiment is enough for us all. There is memory of beauty, there is the survival and rebirth of our people and there remains the carrier of our tradition and commitment, whether we choose it or not. This is because our chosenness is a "given," only to be reformulated in each new age and clime. My father has expressed it for us all. I am reminded of the story told by some famous European writer who heard that there were Jews who were not religious. He could not believe it, for the essence of the Jew, he thought, was the intense, personal and communal connection with God. This non-Jew understood us better than we understand ourselves.

NOTES

1. van der Leeuw, Gerhard, *Religion in Essence and Manifestation*, George Allen & Unwin Ltd., London, 1938 (original in 1933), 709 pp.

2. Spiegelman, J. Marvin and Miyuki, Mokusen, *Buddhism and Jungian Psychology*, Falcon Press, Phoenix, 1985.

3. Spiegelman, J. Marvin, "Psychotherapy and the Clergy: Fifty Years later," *Journal of Religion and Health*, Vol. 23, #1, 1984, pp. 19-32

4. Jung, C.G., *Memories, Dreams, Reflections*, Pantheon Books, Random House, New York, 1961. 368 pp.

5. Spiegelman, J. Marvin, *Essay on Utopia*, on file at C.G. Jung Institute in Zurich, Switzerland, Chicago, Illinois and Los Angeles, California. 1958.198 pp.

6. Jung C.G., *Modern Man in Search of a Soul*, Kegan Paul, London, 1933.

7. Spiegelman, J. Marvin, *The Tree: Tales in Psycho-Mythology*, Phoenix House, Los Angeles, 1975. Reprinted in paper-back by Falcon Press, Phoenix, 1982.

8. H. Sperling, translator, *The Zohar*, in five volumes. Soncino Press, London, 1933.

9. Kluger, Rivkah Schaerf, *Psyche and Bible*, Spring Publications, Zurich, 1974,144 pp.

10. Jung C.G. *Answer to Job*, Collected Works, Vol. 11, Original 1952.

11. Eliade, Mircea, *The Myth of the Eternal Return*, Routledge and Kegan Paul, London, 1955.195 pp.

12. Spiegelman, J. Marvin, "Remembrance of Jung" in Jensen, F., Editor, *C.G. Jung Emma lung and Toni Wolff: Collection of Remembrances*, Analytical Psychology Club of San Francisco, 1982, pp. 86-89.

13. See note number 7.

14. One might ask how can a Knight be Jewish? And I would answer, in Passover fashion, that this is how this Knight differs from all other Knights!

15. Spiegelman, J. Marvin, *The Quest: Further Tales in Psycho-Mythology*, Falcon Press, Phoenix, 1984,175 plus x pp.

16. Spiegelman, J. Marvin, *The Love*, to be published in 1986-7.

17. Soloveitchik, Rabbi Joseph B., *Halakhic Man*, Jewish Publication Society of America, Philadelphia, 1983, pp. 164.

18. Soloveitchik, Rabbi Joseph, "The Lonely Man of Faith," *Tradition*, Summer 1965, 5, 5-67.

19. Greenberg, Blu, On Woman and Judaism, *A View from Tradition*, Jewish Publication Society of America, Philadelphia, 1981, pp. 178.

20. See note 10.

21. In my psychomythological tales in *The Tree* and *The Quest* and most particularly in *The Love*.

PART II: DISHARMONY

THE JEWISH UNDERSTANDING OF EVIL IN THE LIGHT OF JUNG'S PSYCHOLOGY

(A Lecture presented at the Conference of Psychology and Judaism, Cedars-Sinai Medical Center, February, 1988 and at C.G. Jung Institute, Los Angeles, Fall, 1991)

INTRODUCTION

Jews may be said to be specialists in the "Problem of Evil," having undergone intense persecution at the hands of Christian and Moslem civilizations, as well as indignity, harassment, defeat, slavery and death from other cultures, such as the Romans, the Assyrians, the Babylonians, and the Egyptians. Indeed, one origin of the name of "Hebrew" has it that it derives from a word meaning "driven across" a river. From the outset, we Jews have been hounded by others and, what is more, by God Himself! That is what it has meant to be a Chosen People. This "chosenness" has set Jews apart and has both caused and resulted in a separateness which has led to both pain and achievement.

In a sense, then, Jews have no cause to even consider the question of "theodicy"—namely, how can a good God countenance evil?—since good and evil, in our tradition, comes from God Himself. As the great prophet Isaiah has conveyed to us (Isa. 45: 5-7) God proclaimed: "I am the Lord, and there is none else... I form the light and create darkness; I make peace and create evil; I, the Lord, do all these things."

Our fierce monotheism, an achievement enduring more than three millennia, would militate against the acceptance of there being two principles in the cosmos, as is experienced and formulated in other religions and is obvious to other monotheisms who know full well that the evil principle runs rampant through existence. We are not blind to evil, however, as, perhaps, animals are. These fellow creatures, unlike our ancestors Adam and Eve, are totally subservient to God's will and live and die with no sense of injustice. We Jews—and we humans—do complain and cry out about evil.

Could one not ask, "How can it be that there is so much good in the world, given that people, in the main, are indifferent, self-serving, often cruel, and that Nature, under God, is relentlessly unmerciful?" (Levi Meier

61

raises a similar question in his paper of 1981). We normally do not ask such a question, since we seem to linger on in holding beliefs that the world and life ought to be primarily "good." Is this from the bliss of early childhood's "good-enough" parenting, as Winicott might say, or from the racial memory of Paradise before we got expelled? I do not know. But we clearly are gifted with that potential for questioning and even expectation. For, if God chose us, then we must have had some merit, or at least we gain it by virtue of the choice itself. Such a divine figure, complete with omniscience and omnipotence, must have had good reasons for doing so. Therefore, we think that we ought to be treated better.

It was not always so. Whether or not we think that the Bible is the literal word of God or not, it is clearly a document which developed over time and contains within it the record of consciousness evolving, showing a changing perspective and understanding of our images of God Himself and of humankind's relationship to Him. So, therefore, the problem of evil and the presentation of the character of Satan, who is one of its representatives in the Bible, undergoes considerable differentiation during the course of the work. This has been ably demonstrated by Rivkah Schaerf-Kluger in her book, *Satan And The Old Testament* (1967).

I shall summarize Kluger's research later on, but here I want to contrast the presentation of evil as it first appears in Genesis, in the form of that demonic serpent who encouraged our ancestors to taste of the knowledge of good and evil, with the full presentation of Satan as the "adversary" of God and man in the story of Job. In the earlier instance, God instructs the first pair to enjoy everything except that famous tree. They take the first opportunity to disobey, of course, just like any child. We can assume that God was either a poor psychologist who ought to have known better or, in His omniscience, knew what He was doing, wanting and needing us to have freedom of choice or—and here is the viewpoint that I will be espousing later on—that He both knew and did not know. It is this ambivalence of our God-image that we will be examining henceforth. In order to grasp such a viewpoint, I shall review two contributions by Jungians. Before I do so, I shall summarize the Jewish understanding of the problem of evil, from both the normative and mystical points of view.

EVIL FROM THE POINT OF VIEW OF NORMATIVE JUDAISM

For the normative viewpoint, we will draw on some of the classic texts in the field, such as that of George Foote Moore, *Judaism In the First Centuries of the Christian Era. The Age of the Tannaim* (1966), Eliezer Berkovits, *God, Man and History* (1965), and the more recent book of Ephraim E. Urbach, *The Sages: Their Concepts and Beliefs* (1979).

Berkovits reminds us that in the classical Jewish viewpoint, perfection resides in God alone. The world is apart from God and, therefore, imperfect. If it were perfect, it would extinguish itself by tumbling back into God (p.76). God is an Absolute beyond all opposites and attributes. He only "acquires these attributes in the act of self-denial by which He creates the world, to which he relates Himself... So (like Isaiah), we may say, only by creating darkness can God form the light; only through the creation can peace be made (p.79)." The imperfection in the world, therefore, is the source of man's freedom and is both a challenge and an opportunity for human beings to perfect it and themselves.

Moore adds the understanding that evil is not just an opportunity, but it is also a consequence of man's freedom. "The impulses which prompt a man to do or say or think things contrary to the revealed will of God is comprehensively named, *yezer hara*, the evil impulse" (p.479). Man was created with this impulse by God. It is present from the outset of life, and is a consequence of the freedom to choose (p. 479). The way to avoid this evil is to follow the word and law of God. This evil impulse can be personified and identified with Satan, which it was, in later periods (p. 492). Evil is connected with sin, which is defined as any departure from the divine rule of life, whether in morals or religious observance, deliberate or unwitting (p. 493). Everyone sins, of course, but redemption is possible by ritual atonement, repentance and God's forgiveness.

From the foregoing, we can see that in classical Jewish understanding, man, unlike God, is a duality, not a single union. He has both good and bad impulses, is both spirit and flesh. He is like both angels and animals, yet is unlike both. The body itself is not evil, since the soul and body are meant to be in union. There are Talmudic stories which show that both soul and body are to be blamed for evil, but I would like us to be aware that the problem of duality is here handed over to the human being, with his dual impulses, while God remains whole. We shall expatiate on this theme later on.

Urback adds to our understanding of the function of evil in Jewish life by drawing on the words of Rabbi Akiba, who told us that "suffering is precious" (p.445). When the great Rabbi was being tried by the wicked Tineius Rufus for stubbornly following Jewish law, he recited the *Shema*, knowing full well that this was punishable by death. When queried about this act, he said that the verse, "Thou shalt love the Lord thy God with all thy heart and with all thy soul and with all thy might" could now finally be embraced by him in its totality. For the first time he had the chance to face the ordeal of loving God, in the face of death, "with all my soul." It was this that enabled him to recite the *Shema* with great joy.

Not only does this suffering of evil with consciousness and love help redeem a person, it is pointed out that this also brings salvation to the world. The sage Rabbi Meir, for instance, said, "The evil inclination ceases to be evil—it even becomes good—when it is possible for a man to love the Lord with both his inclinations—with the good and the bad (p.475)." The implication is that he who fights and refuses to surrender to his evil inclination transforms it and, therefore, shows his love of God. That this has collective significance, that even the world is redeemed thereby, shows a psychological understanding which has only been grasped in contemporary times. This parallel with the psychological findings of Jung will be seen later on.

But God did not only create the evil inclination. It is as if he said (p.472): "My children, I have created for you the Evil inclination, but I have at the same time created the Torah as an antidote. As long as you occupy yourselves with the Torah it shall not have dominion over you." Yet men do have special prayers to God, asking for help in the conquest of evil. Some say that the good God did not create evil but "put the evil leaven in the dough." For the fermentation of this evil, man alone is responsible.

So much for man's evil and what he can do about it. What about when it appears that god Himself does evil, for instance when He required that Amalek be totally obliterated, the innocent women and children as well as the warriors? When Saul protested about this, we recall the Lord responded, "Be not righteous overmuch" (p.518). This injunction of the Lord for the human being not to overstep himself is a wisdom also shown in fairy tales. Von Franz (1974) demonstrates that it is oftentimes not wise to be confrontative about evil emanating from the Most High. We shall have to consider this in some more depth later on.

We can end this summary of the classical Jewish understanding of evil with our recognition of the ambivalence suggested: God is the source of both good and evil; man is both responsible and benevolent victim. One answer to this ambivalence is given us by David, that great sinner beloved by God, who expressed best the sense that for us Jews it is the ongoing relationship with God which is the answer to evil. In Psalm xxiii, he said:

> Yea, though I walk through the valley of the shadow of death, I will fear no evil, for Thou art with me.

EVIL FROM THE VIEWPOINT OF JEWISH MYSTICISM

We can now examine the approach of Jewish mysticism to the problem of evil. For this, naturally, we draw on the work of Gershom Sholem (1964, 1965) as well as the classic primary source, the *Zohar* (1956).

The *Zohar*, the colorful text of the thirteenth century which is itself an outgrowth and flowering of hundreds of years of speculation, sees evil as having two sources, the one human and the other divine. Both bases of evil, however, rest on the same fundamental failure or destructiveness, namely the separation of things which ought to be together or the union of that which ought to be kept separate. Sin, for example, always destroys a union, and is connected with the original transgression. Not only did Adam and Eve disobey, but more importantly, there was a separation of the Tree of Knowledge from the Tree of Life. Thus, in psychological terms, consciousness is thereby separated from the flow of organic life. This implies that if man violates the fundamental and basic order of all things, as well as his place in that order, the result is a kind of hubris of his own power, putting himself in the place of God. That is the basic condition of human evil: arrogating power to ourselves which is not ours, and thus causing a split in what has been united. In Jungian psychology, we understand that as identifying with an archetype, or *inflation*.

A still deeper understanding in the *Zohar* of the causes of evil is to be found in the character of the divine itself. Kabbalah sees the totality of divine potencies as forming a harmonious whole, and as long as there is such a relation of the opposites to each other in this fashion, it is sacred and good. When, however, this harmony is unbalanced, evil results. For example, the wrath of God, symbolized by His left hand, is connected with strict justice, rigor and judgment. The love and mercy of God, however, is symbolized by his right hand. When the one tempers the other, goodness prevails. When stern judgment, on the other hand, ceases to be balanced, evil results. When it ceases to be tempered altogether, when it tears itself loose from the quality of mercy, then it is transformed into the radically evil, into Gehenna and the dark world of Satan. Evil, therefore, is understood at this level as the *hypertrophy of God's wrath.*

It is notable that this doctrine is not dissimilar to the ideas of the great Christian philosopher Jacob Boehme (1575-1624), who was apparently familiar with Kabbalistic thought. Indeed, it seems to me that just as Jewish Kabbalah was influenced by Christianity, particularly the idea of the Trinity, and by Hindu thought, the result also fed back into Christian mysticism.

In Zoharic understanding, it is clear that evil has two sources, as I have said, both human and divine. These intermingle. The primary source, however, lies in the divine itself. Evil fell into the world not only because Adam's fall actualized its presence, but it has its own reality, independent of man. It is in the nature of the existence of God. This understanding presents the image of evil as a residue of the life process of God Himself. God is seen as a living organism, so that just a tree cannot exist without its bark, or the human body without shedding "unclean" detritus, thus the demonic has its root in the mystery of God's existence. In later Kabbalism, evil is seen as the *Kelipah* or the "bark" of the cosmic tree, or the "shell" of the nut. We shall pursue this in the later work of Luria, but we can conclude our presentation of the Zoharic view of evil as espousing the position that evil has its ordained place, but is itself not alive; it comes to life only because a ray of light, however faint, comes from the holiness of God and falls upon this potential. It is quickened by man's sin, and is itself part of the dark side of everything living. The resemblance of this view to that of Jung will occupy us later, but now we turn to the further emendations of the Kabbalistic philosophy in the great Isaac Luria of Safed.

Luria (1534-1578) expanded from the original view of creation understood as: (1) God projecting His creative power out of His own Self into space, and each act as a further stage in the process of externalization; (2) in the Zohar as God having concentrated his *Shekinah*, his divine feminine presence, into a single point. Luria uses the word *tsimtsum*, concentration or contraction, not as concentration *at* a point, but retreat *away* from a point. This means that the universe, in which God is everywhere, is made possible by the voluntary removing of Himself from a space in order to return to it in the act of creation and revelation. He thus concentrated Himself unto Himself, as the first act. This profound seclusion, *tsimtsum*, is a deep symbol of Exile, or separation. The first act is limitation; only the second act is creation; and this is the pattern of every cosmic process.

According to this view, before the *tsimtsum* took place, the essence of the Divine Being contained not only love and mercy, but also sternness and judgment, called *Din*. Before creation, this was not recognizable as such, but was dissolved in the great ocean of God's compassion. In the act of *tsimtsum*, however, it crystallized and became defined as an act of negation, limitation and judgment. It is in this that evil begins. It is necessary because without limitation there are no boundaries, hence no individuality. But limitation—and its transgression—brings in the possibility of evil. Existence, therefore, always includes two aspects, ebb and flow, *hithpashtuth* (egression) and *histalkuth* (regression). The universe itself, like the organism, exists through a double process of inhalation and exhalation.

Along with this conception of the origin of evil in the cosmic process, Luria introduced two other major ideas which clarify this understanding of evil in Jewish thought, along with the idea of the reparation of that same evil. The first idea is that of *Shevirath Ha-Kelem*, or the "Breaking of the Vessels" and the second is that of *Tikkun* or the mending of a defect. The "breaking" occurred in the original acts of creation when the divine light shattered the special containers that were meant to hold it. As the grandeur of the Divine Being gradually manifested into the sephiroth or vessels to contain it, the light was too much and fracture occurred. This fracture, however, according to Luria's followers, was also connected with the law of organic life, Just as the seed must burst in order to blossom, so too, the vessels that contained divine light had to burst so that creation could occur. In this way, however, good elements of the divine order were mixed with evil ones and the restoration of the ideal order is the secret purpose of existence. Salvation, therefore, means restitution, re-integration of the original whole, or *tikkun* in Hebrew. The process is one whereby the "sparks" of the divine, as they are called, are recovered from their fall into creation.

The crucial element in this doctrine of repair or healing of the process of evil, in our connection, is that this *tikkun* requires the participation of humankind. The mystical creator of all things needs the human being to help recover the sparks and lights. This process is even described as the "birth of God's personality," and has an historical aspect to it. The historical process itself, and its most important aspects, derives from religious acts, which pave the way for the final restitution of all the scattered and exiled lights and sparks. The Jew who is in close contact with the divine life through Torah, the fulfillment of the commandments, and through prayer, had it in his power to accelerate or hinder this process, "Every act of man is related to this final task which God has set for His creatures"(p.274).

It follows from this that the appearance of the messiah is nothing but the consummation of this restoration, of *Tikkun*. The task of man is seen as directing his whole purpose, his mystical intention of *kawwannah* towards restoring the original harmony which was disturbed by the Breaking of the Vessels, from which the powers of evil and sin began. This is understood as "unifying the name of God," to join the latter two letters of the holy name of God with the first two, of WH joining with JH, in the tetragrammaton. Exile is repaired and brokenness redeemed. God is restored to Himself, mankind with God, and the union of the feminine, *Shekinah*, with the masculine. This, itself, is a manifestation of Messiah. Each person, therefore, carries responsibility for the Messianic task. The way is *Kawwanah*, mystical intention, to *Devekuth,*, mystical contact with God, which produces a *unio mystica*. The resemblance to alchemical ideas in this conception is profound.

R. SCHAERF-KLUGER'S WORK

We turn now, to the understanding of evil from the Jungian point of view. First, we shall examine the work of Rivkah Schaerf-Kluger, who received her doctoral degree in Semitic Languages and Religious History from the University of Zurich and was trained as an Analyst by C.G. Jung. She has resided in Israel for a number of years. Her seminal research on *Satan and the Old Testament* (1967) first appeared in German in 1948. Her book, therefore, antedates Jung's monumental work, *Answer to Job* (1958), which first appeared in 1952. Both of these books were written only a few years after the horrors of the Holocaust were revealed to the world. They are unique in that they take up the question of the changes in our images of God and Man that such a cataclysmic event demands. Indeed, in my opinion, there has been little since then to compare with either these two works.

Schaerf-Kluger begins by showing that the monotheism of the Old Testament reveals an ambivalent God-image, mingling light and dark, good and evil, in one divine personality. This monotheism, then, is a *unity of multiplicity* (p.10), a combination of many aspects. As an example, let me point out that one of the names of God, *Elohim,* is a plural noun which appears right at the outset of Genesis, when the Lord as Creator is designated in that form. Schaerf-Kluger says that her aim is to show that this development into a single personality is an outstanding achievement in the Old Testament, in which the concept of Satan has an important role. This Satan, who in much later Judaism is equivalent with the "evil impulse" in the human soul (*yezer hara,*) appears first as merely an opposition, as an "adversary" or "hinderer" (pp. 38-39). In the story of David, for example, we see what is happening in his human soul as a reflection of what is going on in the divine sphere. The mal'ak Yahweh (spirit of God) commands Satan—who is clamoring for the punishment of Joshua—to be silent, just as David commands the silence of the sons of Zeruiah. There is no meeting of the metaphysical and human realms here, however.

With the story of Balaam, however, it is no longer a conflict in the divine realm, but it is an *angel* who stands in the way of Balaam, the human being. Here, the mal'ak Yahweh is an adversary. "That which crosses human plans and wishes comes from the divine sphere" (p. 38). Satan here, as in the preceding passages, is not yet a mythological figure, but a functional concept, hindering. In the story of Job, a further step is shown in that the adversary is not merely God's messenger; "he stands over against God in a dialectical relation." He has become a personal figure in the divine realm. In short, Satan is a personified function of God, which develops step by step and detaches itself from the divine personality (p.52).

From Dr. Kluger's presentation, we can see that there is a steady development of the "hindering," adversarial function in the divine image to something independent and far-reaching; this attains its ultimate in Christianity. This same mal'ak Yahweh, who in II Kings (19:35) slays 185,000 Assyrians in one night without remorse, undergoes a different fate in II Samuel (24:16), where it says :

> And when the angel stretched out his hand upon Jerusalem to destroy it, Yahweh repented him of the evil, and said to the angel that destroyed the people: It is enough; stay now thy hand.

Schaerf-Kluger remarks (p.70) that

> The mal'ak Yahweh is therefore the instrument for carrying out the divine will, the activity of God, but it is as if there arose a conflict in God, which is followed by an inner change; he repents his stern judgment. He is no longer identical with his destructive function; he opposes it by commanding the mal'ak Yahweh to stay his hand. Here we have already a confrontation within God Himself which takes more pronounced form in the later scriptures.

In the story of Balaam and the she-ass, God appears as both helpful and threatening. He blocks Balaam's path, threatening death, but also helps him to see so that he can obey. As Schaerf-Kluger puts it, "God puts himself in man's path in order to hinder him, but his purpose is that man comes up against him, becomes aware of his presence." The psychological interpretation of this event is that the human will becomes conscious only through its collision with the divine will, the adversary. Thus, behind the divine deadly threat there is a positive, purposeful aspect: the creation of greater consciousness.

I would add that there is simultaneously presented the need for both consciousness and submission, just as there was in Eden, but now there is more realization on both sides, God's and man's. If this kind of reasoning seems strange, think of the statement of Yahweh in Job 2:3, wherein God speaks to Satan as follows: "Thou movest me against him to destroy him without cause." An old Talmud teacher remarked about this passage that "If it were not in the Bible, one would not be allowed to say it", for God is represented "like a man who lets himself be seduced by another" (p.82).

In the next chapter of Schaerf-Kluger's work, she considers Satan as one of the *bene-ha-elohim*, such as Leviathan and Behemoth, the mythological figures representing the wild-nature side of Yahweh. She shows that Satan is "not himself the dark nature force symbolized in all these images; he is rather a spiritual differentiating principle in God which caused God to become aware of his own nature side" (p.87)

These same *bene-ha-elohim*, who taught man the arts and sciences, in Genesis 6:1-4, separate from God and perform an act on their own, even contrary to His will. They say "the daughters of men that they were fair; and they took them wives of all which they chose." Schaerf-Kluger points out that they thus represent an independent impulse, a desire to unite with human kind. Psychologically, this expresses a still "unconscious urge in God toward men, which is also suggested by the multiplicity of the angels as aspects of God. It is not a conscious inclining of God toward men, as in the later theologem of God becoming man, but an unconscious urge. Therefore the union does not result, as it does later, in a God-man, but in monsters." From this reasoning, we can conclude that there is a side of God which wants to unite with man, and a side which does not, since this would make man an equal to God.

Now we may recall that in the very beginning, God expelled humankind from Eden, lest they partake of the Tree of Life and "become as one of us." This profound and cryptic remark will occupy us later, but here we must note, once more, that there is an ambivalent tendency apparent in the Most High: to both include humankind in its process and to exclude it. Without giving away our hypothesis altogether, we can say at this point that the divine seems to need both aspects of us: to grow in independence and choice and to be connected and united; sometimes these needs conflict in both God and man.

As we continue, now, with Schaerf-Kluger's argument, she shows us in the next part that in the Book of Job, the *bene-ha-elohim* are no longer an undivided multiplicity, but that one among them, Satan, takes on a particular function (p.119): "He is an independent active side of God, who is in conflict with God's total personality, and by whose opposing will God is perturbed. God accepts this side of himself and lets it have its way; yet he is critical and uncertain about it." Satan is God's "overseer" of men, which is born of the *el-qanna*—the jealous God of Exodus, who is suspicious of His people. With Job, however, he is different. Schaerf-Kluger expresses it well, as follows (p.119):

> Whereas elsewhere in the Old Testament God demands unbroken piety and flares into wrath only when he does not meet with it, here Job's obedience does not satisfy him. There lurks in him a secret doubt which in Satan, the separate side of his being, is manifested fully.

We conclude that *Satan functions here as the manifested doubt of God*. He devaluates Job's piety and caused God to deliver Job up to him. Our impulsive, wrathful divinity has appeared frequently earlier on, such as with Noah, with whom he made an "everlasting covenant" and gave us the rainbow so that *He* would remember it. Somewhat similarly, the temptation of Abraham shows us that God was willing to risk the whole plan of salvation and His creation, in order to assure Himself of Abraham's piety.

Rabbi Emil Fackenheim, however, reports a conversation with a young Hassid from Brooklyn which sheds a different light on the *Akedah* (1986, p.15). The young scholar was of the opinion that the reason God personally told Abraham to sacrifice Isaac but only sent an angel for the reprieve was that the Almighty was "fed up" with Abraham; he wanted him to say "No" in the first place! This story is a pleasant personal Midrash but it also sheds light on the theme I am dealing with here: God seems to want man to both stand up for himself and to submit as well!

With Job things changed. God had been aware of His own wrathful nature. With Moses, for example (Exodus 33:3), He says, "I will not go up in the midst of thee; for thou art a stiff-necked people: lest I consume thee on the way." He has been unpredictable, but as a fact, not a problem. In God's speeches to Job it becomes a problem, since God consciously admits the darkness in Himself and wants it to be seen and accepted by man. Job's greatness is that he does so; he bows to the irrational God: "I have heard of thee by the hearing of the ear: but now mine eye seeth thee" (Job 42: 5,6).

Dr. Kluger informs us that she learned from Jung the following understanding of this final speech:

God reveals himself to Job in all his frightfulness. It is as if he said to Job: 'Look, that is what I am like. That is why I treated you like this'. Through the suffering which he inflicted upon Job out of his own nature, God has come to this self-knowledge and admits, as it were, this knowledge of his frightfulness to Job. *And that is what redeems the man Job* (p.129).

Out of this experience, Job, a man who previously lived a satisfied existence of unreflected piety, is transformed into one *who accepts not only the good God, but also the dark one,* and through it all, he is able to proclaim a deeper connection with the goodness, when he says, "I know that my redeemer liveth." He is expanded in consciousness and couples this extended knowledge with submission to God as well. The knowledge is fruitful only when accompanied by submission, otherwise there is the hubris that God feared—"lest they become as one of us."

Kluger shows us, furthermore, that the Job story shows an accompanying advance of God, psychologically speaking. In Paradise, He seemed to know so little of why He created mankind that He cast them away because of their knowledge of good and evil. Now, in Job, Satan, unlike the serpent, brings the "evil" idea up directly. We also see that Satan's function in the Book of Job is to be a foe of the peaceful life and worldly comfort. *He brings consciousness to God, as well as to man.* Two aspects of God fight over man, one wanting to annihilate him, the other to save him. One side wants justice, the other grants mercy. The release of the one is followed by the other. The "satanic" element is part of the plan of salvation: the adversary of God brings about consciousness and a higher level of union. Thus the function of Satan, and his final, urgent goal, is to "make the human soul the dwelling place of God becoming conscious of himself" (p.162).

JUNG'S "ANSWER TO JOB"

When we turn, now, to Jung's monumental work, *Answer to Job* (1958), we are faced with what I believe to be a turning point in the history of religion. It is not prophecy or revelation in the usual sense, but the application of the highest development of contemporary consciousness. That is to say, Jung is critical, objective and penetrating as a scientist and scholar, but along with this he brings emotion, subjectivity and, above all, piety. The work is nothing less than a psychological approach to the image of the divine in western civilization as it has developed over several thousand years. It addresses itself specifically to our present question, the problem of good and evil. The occasion for beginning this work had to do with Jung's quarrel with the Christian understanding of God as only goodness, the *summum bonum*, with evil merely as the *privatio boni*, the lack of good. This viewpoint, he believed, was in total disagreement with the findings about the nature of the psyche itself. This hearkens back to the tremendous religious problem of how the images of God are to be understood. All these images point to a union of opposites in the God image, and recall the fundamental story of Job, who "expected help from God against God." Jung undertook the task of examining this problem in its historical evolution from the time of Job down to the most recent symbolic phenomena, such as the Papal doctrine of the *assumptio Mariae*, the bodily elevation of Mary into heaven.

The basis for Jung's work, he tells us, lies in the modern understanding that religious statements are psychic in origin, tell us about the psyche and its functioning, particularly its most important, fundamental and archetypal basis, and about the collective development of religious consciousness. The *images* of God are what are examined, with no claim to being able to assert eternal truths about the Unknowable or to prove any metaphysical statements. The distinction is between *physical* truth, which religious statements are not, and *psychological* truth, which they are.

As I attempted to summarize Jung's work for our present purposes, I found myself taking voluminous notes, covering eight legal-sized pages of foolscap for a book only 113 pages in length. Since many in this audience are not likely to have read this work, I shall be generous in my summary, but urge us all, particularly Jews and Christians, to study it.

To give the flavor of Jung's writing style in this unusual volume, I will quote the first paragraph of it after the introduction (1958, par. 560):

> The book of Job is a landmark in the long historical development of a divine drama. At the time the book was written, there were already many testimonies which had given a contradictory picture of Yahweh—the picture of a God who knew no moderation in his emotions and suffered precisely from this lack of moderation. He himself admitted that he was eaten up with rage and jealousy and that this knowledge was painful to him. Insight existed along with cruelty, creative power along with destructiveness Everything was there, and none of these qualities was an obstacle to the other. Such a condition is only conceivable either when no reflecting consciousness is present at all, or when the capacity for reflection is very feeble and a more or less adventitious phenomenon. A condition of this sort can only be described as amoral.

So does Jung begin. His astonishing insight gives a Jew like me pause and makes one aware that this same god image was He who brought in and demanded the highest level of moral attainment that was possible in the ancient world. Soon we are faced with the power of this divine antinomy and the experience of it in Job, whose greatest quality, says Jung, is that "he does not doubt the unity of God." He clearly sees that God is at odds with himself—so flatly at odds that he, Job, is quite certain of finding in God a helper, an "advocate" against God. As certain as he is of the evil in Yahweh, he is equally certain of the good (par. 567). God is a personality and tremendously involved with humankind, in contrast with the all-ruling Father Zeus, who "in a benevolent and somewhat detached manner" allows the universe to go along, and only punishes the disorderly. The Greek God did not moralize but ruled instinctively, demanding only the sacrifices due him; he was not involved overmuch with human beings, having no plans for them. The Jewish God needed human beings, and swore to David, for instance in the 89th Psalm, that he would not lie to him. Yet he "who watched so jealously over the fulfillment of laws and contracts, broke his own oath" (par. 570). This is an image of a being who lacks self-reflection. He is not imperfect or evil, like a Gnostic demiurge, but is everything in its totality; thus he is totally justice s well as its total opposite.

Why then, does God need man? He needs humankind for a greater consciousness, a more precise rendering of Himself to Himself. Yet he is ambivalent about this, abandons His faithful servant, Job, to evil, who thereby is secretly lifted up to a superior knowledge which God Himself does not possess, namely His own antinomy. Yet we discover that Job is an outward occasion for an inward dialectic in God Himself (par. 587). It is as if God projects his own skepticism on Job, and the latter is challenged as though he, himself, were a god!

Man is enormously elevated thereby, something that has never happened before, because "without knowing it or wanting it, a mortal man is raised by his moral behavior above the stars in heaven, from which position of advantage he can behold the back of Yahweh, the abysmal world of 'shards'". Jung is referring here to the idea in Kabbalah that the shards or "shells" are counterpoles to the ten *sephiroth* or stages in the revelation and manifestation of God's creative power. The shards represent the forces of evil and darkness, which are a by-product of the process of the *sephiroth*. We shall speak more of this later on.

Job has discovered that God is a phenomenon, "not a man"—even less than human in some ways. Jung points out that to assume that the creator of the world is a conscious being is a disastrous prejudice which leads to such nonsensical doctrines as the *privatio boni*. "Divine unconsciousness and lack of reflection, on the other hand, enable us to form a conception of God which puts his actions beyond moral judgment and allows no conflict to arise between goodness and beastliness" (footnote, p.383).

Job reacts in an adjusted way, but sees that Yahweh behaves as irrationally as a cataclysm and then "wants to be loved, honored, worshipped and praised as just... One can submit to such a God only with fear and trembling...but a relationship of trust is out of the question to our modern way of thinking." Yet Yahweh demands loyalty and gets it. By humiliating Job, however, he pronounces judgment on himself and gives man moral satisfaction which is not recognized. This could have resulted in the relativization that effected the Greek Gods, but this did not happen for the next two thousand years. Yet God's dual nature was perceived by the unconscious mind of man and was bound to have far-reaching consequences.

At this point in Jung's discussion, he makes a *discursus* back to the time when the Book of Job was written, sometime between 600 and 300 B.C.E., which places it also about the time of the Book of Proverbs. He does so in order to further assess what was happening in the psyche about this time, when the far-reaching effect of Job was occurring. He thereby demonstrates the natural process of the development of the idea of the "incarnation" and the emergence of the Christian story. Thus far, I imagine, I have maintained the connection with my fellow Jews during this presentation of Jung's reflections, but now a further step is needed. We need now to understand, psychologically, the sequence which led to the modern era, via Christianity. If Jews might tend to leave the presentation at this point, let me ask them to maintain interest since the discussion is a psychological one and is one of the few, in my experience, that makes the idea of a historical Judeo-Christian continuum both sensible and palatable, doing damage to neither religious outlook.

The Book of Proverbs shows the effect of Greek influence, in that the idea of Sophia, the *Sapientia Dei* or Wisdom of God, is presented as a feminine spirit which existed before Creation. This Sophia is a part of God with characteristics like the Johannine *Logos*, the *Chochma* of Kabbalah, but also the Indian *Shakti*. This feminine Wisdom is exalted as the Word of God ("I come out of the mouth of the most High"). As *Ruach*, she brooded over the waters at the beginning, and has her throne in heaven. In the apocryphal Wisdom of Solomon, she is wisdom as a loving spirit, "kind to man." She is also said to be "better than might." We already know how the Book of Job revealed God in his relationship to power. Now hear Jung as he describes what could have happened psychologically during this period (par. 616):

> From the ancient records we know that the divine drama was enacted between God and his people, who were betrothed to him, the masculine dynamis, like a woman, and over whose faithfulness he watched jealously. A particular instance of this is Job, whose faithfulness is subjected to a savage test... The really astonishing thing is how easily Yahweh gives in to the insinuations of Satan. If it were true that he trusted Job perfectly, it would be logical for Yahweh to defend him, unmask the malicious slanderer, and make him pay for his defamation of God's faithful servant... But Yahweh never thinks of it, not even after Job's innocence has been proved. We hear nothing of a rebuke or disapproval of Satan. Therefore, one

cannot doubt Yahweh's connivance. His readiness to deliver Job into Satan's murderous hands proves that he doubts Job precisely because he projects his own tendency to unfaithfulness upon a scape-goat. There is reason to suspect that he is about to loosen his matrimonial ties with Israel but hides this intention from himself.

Jung shows that, with the help of Satan, God infallibly picks on the most faithful of the lot, Job. At about the same time, God remembers a feminine being who was a friend and playmate from the beginning of the world, the first-born of all his creatures, a "stainless reflection of his glory and a master workman," namely Sophia. There must be some dire necessity for this anamnesis of Sophia: things simply could not go on as before, the 'just' God could not go on committing injustices, and the 'Omniscient' could not behave any longer like a clueless and thoughtless human being. Self-reflection becomes imperative, and for this Wisdom is needed. We thus realize that the failure to corrupt Job has induced changes in Yahweh's nature.

EXCURSUS ON JESUS AND THE GOD-MAN IDEA

In my original summary of Jung's book, *Answer to Job*, the part wherein Jung describes the psychological evolution and significance of the incarnation, or God-Man idea, seemed to be fraught with gravity for some Jewish readers. And these latter were by no means unenlightened with regard to Jung, nor narrow-minded. It was just that the very consideration of Jesus, in a Jewish context, let alone with the God-Man conception, brought on resistance and even revulsion for some, on the basis of the anti-Semitic history of Christianity. The name and image of Jesus had so often been used as an instrument of oppression that the mere mentioning of the name, in a Jewish context, brought on the resistance. This occurred, I discovered, even among some Jews who were in Jungian training; they were unable to continue reading Jung's book when the image of Jesus came into play. This happened despite their understanding that Jung's approach was psychological, that he even was highly critical of the Christian viewpoint of *summum bonum* and that he, like most contemporary scholars (even Christian theologians) did not see Jesus as other than a Jewish reformer.

In short, in considering the problem of evil from a Jewish point of view, we have come up against an image of evil in the figure of Jesus himself! This is a mirror-image of the Christian view of the Jews, having rejected Jesus as son of God puts them in league with the Devil! I, therefore, had to pause in my presentation to take up this issue itself.

Lest one might think that I see myself as free from this prejudice—as some might call it—or reflexive reaction at least, I must report another recent incident which showed me that I was in the same boat. I attended a concert not long ago at which many "Jews for Jesus" were present at the entrance, thrusting their pamphlets at us. Without reflection, I said to one burly fellow who so accosted me, "You ought to be ashamed of yourself!" He answered, also reflexively, "You ought to be ashamed of yourself!" I think that we were both right. I was right from my point of view since I objected not only to one who had apparently betrayed his origins but who was also insensitively missionarizing for his faith. And he was right in that I should be ashamed of condemning someone who was merely preaching as his lights gave them to him. This is still a free country, religiously, thank God, and there is still separation of church and State, so that each of us can follow his or her own myth, own story, own faith. But why, deeply believing this, did I condemn this fellow? Not only for the reasons already mentioned, I think, but because my own myth, my own story, put me in line for such condemnation by others. I was surely no Jew for Jesus, but my own experience in analysis at the end of 1951 was of a dream and vision in which a divine child was being born, not Jesus, but some new figure. Furthermore, this divine child, who was not yet seen and might even have been female, was being attended by three holy men who were an orthodox Jewish rabbi, a Christian priest and a Buddhist priest! Later on, when I read Jung's *Answer to Job* and his *Memoirs*, I fully realized that this "divine child" carried with it a *psychological* viewpoint, one that permitted committed Jews and Christians and Buddhists to *appreciate* the experience of the other paths to the divine as an *inner* event and to see the psyche as developing historically, *without* the loss of one's basic faith.

But others are not so ready to do this. It has even been suggested, if we can give credence to some twin studies reported in the New York Times, that the tendency to fundamentalism and single-minded belief is more genetic than acquired. Even if this is so, how can we apply our psychological understanding to such a situation, particularly in this area of the problem of evil? First of all, I think, it is helpful to recognize that the attribution of evil, the naming of the Satan, is taking place by both parties, those that condemn one if Jesus is not accepted as the Lord, and those who thoughtlessly reject the image itself. It is possible to remember the history of a faith whose members inflicted unspeakable evil on those they condemned as evil without falling into the same condemnation, but it requires a significant act of a discriminating consciousness. Psychologically, it may be helpful to see this evil principle, at work on both sides, as both Judaism and Jung see it, as part of the divine itself.

It is just this confrontation that Jung takes up in his book. He sees the entire development of western civilization, and its religious stories from Egypt and Greece to Jerusalem and Rome, as the expressions of the changing images of God, in accordance with the development of consciousness.

But what is at stake here? What are these extreme opposites that are mutually condemned? The condemnation of the Jews as those who refused to accept Jesus may be a projection of unconscious doubt and uncertainty, but is it not also, as Jung suggests, the very part of the past that Christian development rejected, namely the *union* of good and evil in the divine itself? As Jung says so well, all this protestation of God's goodness, as exemplified in John, was just so much repression of the knowledge of the dark side, to come up blatantly at the end of the Christian Aeon, and repeatedly throughout its history of persecution of Jews.

What does the perceived darkness of the Jesus-image indicate for Jews? Certainly it is the reflexive revulsion from persecution. It is also the historical rejection of what is conceived to be a false Messiah figure. Jews have had their hopes and expectations for such a figure continually dashed, but there is no such antipathy for other "false" messiahs, such as Shabtai Zvi. No, I think that there is more than that here. I think that Jung is right when he suggests the idea of *individuation* in the God-Man image, particularly when one realizes that the psychological direction of the process is toward that same incarnation in the many, ultimately in all of humankind. This individuation, this particularization of the God-image, to reside in the souls of each of us, is a threat to the perception of the God-image as an exclusively collective event, only achievable outwardly and with the established rules. In this viewpoint, fundamentalist Judaism finds its sister in fundamentalist Christianity: there is no salvation outside the Church or *Halacha*.

Can a Jew who respects fundamentalism, both Jewish and Christian, as ways of maintaining something most precious, but who also affirms individuation, find another path in the conflict? I think so. I think it is, as my dream suggested to me, to maintain one's own heritage while remaining open to other experiences of the divine. God speaks in many languages after all. One way to do this is to make use of a psychological viewpoint, which addresses itself to the *psyche* and not those transcendental truths toward which the psyche points and which are acclaimed by faith. This produces conflict, to be sure, but this conflict is part of the individuation process itself, in which the person accepts the opposites and their struggle, one's soul becomes a suitable home for the birth of the divine. This is the proper function of Satan, as Kluger informed us, to provide a dwelling place for God to become conscious of Himself. For those who are friendly to such a view, very well. To those not so inclined, we can bow and nod the head to other images of the divine, including fundamentalism, which also find their place in the soul of humankind.

"But," some might say, "When you suggest that you appreciate Christianity and Buddhism as an inner experience, are you not then no longer a Jew, but a believer in some kind of ecumenical religion, with a psychological flavor?"

My answer to that, in Jewish fashion, is to present a counter question. If I both acknowledge and appreciate the feminine in myself, my anima, and aver a deep and ongoing relationship with her, do I then say that I am no longer a man but a man/woman or some such thing? I do not. I merely acknowledge that my manhood is enriched by my femininity and these aspects, along with others, combine to find their share in that larger totality of my Self. I can even claim that my manhood is more secure by my becoming conscious of my previously unconscious femininity and, therefore, is not vitiated.

One can apply a similar reasoning to all those aspects of one's Self, one's totality, of which one is not conscious: they are projected and often demonized or idealized. When made conscious, they contribute to an awareness of one's totality. So that, greater awareness of my origins and depths, as well as my shadow and rejected sides, makes me more Jewish and certainly more religious than before. For others, I can only suggest that they, too, reflect upon their demons and idealizations.

With this *excursus*, let me return to Jung's presentation of the development in consciousness which led to the God-man idea.

JUNG CONTINUED

Jung carefully traces the early archetypal stories involving the pure son and the impure one. He also reminds us that God did not say "it is good" for the creation of Monday, in which separation of the upper and lower firmament took place. This dualism was not "good." In the pleroma, in the background, there is a perfect interplay of cosmic forces, but with Creation—the division of the world into distinct processes in space and time—conflict occurs. Perfection and completion begin their opposition. We also now discover that Yahweh's marriage with Israel had a perfectionist aim in it, and lacked the kind of relatedness that we now know as "eros." Rather than values and the appreciated subjectivity of the partner, there is only a relationship to a purpose which man must help to fulfill. Faithfulness of his people becomes more important the more he forgets Wisdom.

Job is the climax of this development. Man sees the split in God, needs Wisdom as an advocate. God, having been met and seen, needs her too. Therefore, this realization of Sophia, Wisdom, betokens a coming act of creation, which uses the Egyptian modes of incarnation, in Pharaoh, but this is not merely repeating the archetype mechanically. "The real reason for God's becoming man is to be sought in his encounter with Job" (par. 624).

This time it is not the world that is to be changed. Rather, it is God who intends to change his own nature. Only one human being is to be created, a God-man, born of a human woman, a second Eve. This incarnation was only partial, since it was necessary to protect against evil, and thus he was more divine than human. Therefore, the perfectionism continued. Yet, says Jung (par. 631):

> One should make clear to oneself what it means when God becomes man. It means nothing less than a world shaking transformation of God. It means more or less what Creation meant in the beginning, namely an objectivation of God. At the time of the Creation he revealed himself in nature; now he wants to be more specific and become man.

From this we can understand that God is reality itself. When God created the world from the "void," he breathed his own mystery into every part of it. From this comes the belief that it is possible to know God from his creation (par. 630). If God is in everything already, why the incarnation? One would like to say that Christ had to appear in order to deliver mankind from evil, but, in fact, Yahweh could have simply stopped Satan, if he had wished. Rather what we see—and here is where Jung has touched upon a most profound point which can reconcile us Jews with the idea of the incarnation—is that *God must become man precisely because he has done man a wrong. He, the guardian of justice, knows that every wrong must be expiated, and Wisdom knows that moral law is above even him. Because his creature has surpassed him he must regenerate himself.*

Jung now shows us how the hero myth is invoked in order to bring about the desired experience of the divine who now needs to know what it is like to be a human being. The dove and love-goddess are implied, but the change in the ordinary myth of the hero god dying young is shown by the precise experience of Christ. He is certainly identified with his love of mankind, but the scriptures also reveal a "certain irascibility" in his temperament, as is often the case with people who do not reflect about themselves. The great exception to this lack of questioning himself is found only at the very end, when he cries despairingly on the cross, "my God, my God, why hast thou forsaken me?" Jung now reveals what this means (par. 647):

> Here human nature attains divinity; at that moment God experiences what it means to be a mortal man and drinks to the dregs what he made his faithful servant suffer. Here is given the answer to Job and, clearly, this supreme moment is as divine as it is human, as "eschatological" as it is "psychological."

With this insight, Jung helps us Jews to better comprehend the Christian story and to realize, once again, that religion links us back to myth, and that myth is truth played out, but it is the truth of the psyche. In this myth Satan is also punished at last, but how? He is banished from heaven, not cast directly into hell, however, but is now on earth, as we humans have experienced all along. We shall return to this theme later on. It is enough here for us to see that Yahweh has become the "good" God; but what are we to make of the cautious petition inserted into the prayer: "Lead us not into temptation...?" That, says Jung, is hardly the mark of a divinity who is the *summum bonum*. This theme will continue in the Apocalypse, where Satan incarnates as the dark God.

At this point, Jung contrasts the Catholic and Protestant views, which essentially results in freedom being seen as greater in the latter, but there is more rigidity, too, in that only the Scriptures are regarded as the word of God. Catholicism, with the doctrine of the Holy Ghost, can allow further revelations, such as the important one of the *assumptio Mariae*. Jesus, we are made to see, is not fully human, and it is clear that *God and man suffer from each other* (par. 657), so that in the end the statement "Ye are Gods" can be realized.

The result of this process is that man himself becomes filled with divine conflict, he himself carries the symbol of the cross, which is spirit and flesh, divine and human, in his own being. *It is not God's purpose, apparently, to exempt man from conflict, hence the experience of evil.* Furthermore, Jung asks what kind of father could it be who demands the killing of his first born as a sacrifice? He is surely not the *summum bonum*! As in the Jewish experience, it is healthier to know the opposites, to fear God a well as to love Him.

Now Jung brings in the vision of Ezekiel of the "Higher Man," as well as the experience of the Buddha, in which there is a movement of the divine toward the mortal (the Son of Man) and the reverse. Both God and man want to escape from blind injustice. The central idea in this, Jung states, is as follows (par. 686):

> The inner instability of Yahweh is the prime cause not only of the creation of the world, but also of the pleromatic drama for which mankind serves as a tragic chorus...the two main climaxes are formed first by the Job tragedy and secondly by Ezekiel's revelation.

Job suffers, one might say, but Ezekiel becomes a witness. Enoch becomes a Son of Man in his ecstasy and comes closer also. All these movements culminate, says Jung, in Jesus, who as a Jewish reformer and prophet of an exclusively good God, becomes a sacrifice to reconcile God with Himself and with Man. This incarnation is not confined to the one man, but is presaged as continual.

All this cultivation of good, Jung shows us, is brought to an enantiodromia in the Apocalypse of John (par. 698). He conjectures that the John of the Epistles is the same author as the former, since the continual preaching of goodness brings about the change into darkness shown in the Apocalypse. He also suggests (par. 713) that the more Christian the consciousness, the more heathen will be the unconscious. That very heathen quality such as the image of the divine youth and the beauties of spring, are particularly missing in Christianity, which even developed a denial of sexuality. The chief feature of the visions, however, was not just a personal darkness or shadow of the John of the Apocalypse, but to compensate the too light presentation of the divine. Thus, John's vision extended far beyond the first half of the Christian Aeon of one thousand years. He anticipated the alchemists, Jakob Boheme and, perhaps even sensed God's birth in ordinary man, which the alchemists, Meister Eckhart and Angelus Silesius also intuited (par. 733). The whole outline of the dark ending of the Piscean era is suggested, whose possibilities make mankind shudder. Jung speaks of the four horsemen of the apocalypse, such as the atom bomb, chemical warfare, and the unspeakable destruction of the Holocaust. There is presented the paradoxical idea of God in the apocalypse as both a savior and author in the total universal destruction. In this paradox, God is forcing man to become conscious and unite the forces which assault him. The tendency is to both divide and unite; the need is to assimilate the dark God (pars. 740 and 742).

Everything depends on man, says Jung. "The only thing that really matters now is whether man can climb up to a higher moral level, to a higher plane of consciousness, in order to be equal to the superhuman powers which the fallen angels have played into his hands" (par. 746). In short, man must know the Self, not the little self or ego, but the larger totality of which he is a part. The doctrine of assumption of Mary into heaven points to a *hieros gamos*, a new divine marriage, which will bring about a birth of a divine child in man, which is synonymous with individuation.

Jung points out (in 1952!) that the evolution of consciousness has already indicated a change in that the feminine can no longer be second class, but requires equality. This means that a man's religion (such as Protestantism) is not enough, and that the feminine needs to be represented in the pleroma, which is now taking place. The resulting divine birth means a process in which humankind becomes conscious of its own polarity, divinity and humanity, light and dark, good and evil, in a total and precise way.

The danger in such consciousness, of course, is a terrible inflation, which already exists on the world level among states. The antidote to this inflation of the one who seeks greater consciousness is the realization that:

> Even the enlightened person remains what he is, and is never more than his own limited ego before the One who dwells within him, whose form has no knowable boundaries, who encompasses him on all sides, fathomless as the abysms of the earth and vast as the sky (par. 758, end).

CONCLUSION

Now, having traversed the problem of evil from the normative Jewish viewpoint, from the perspective of Jewish mysticism, and of two representatives of Jungian psychology, it is time for us to sum up, to bring together these diverse strands into some perceptible union. In so doing, we are, as a matter of fact, facing the same task which these diverse views also come up against, namely the problem of unity and multiplicity, of duality and conflict on the one hand, and resolution and harmony on the other.

Perhaps we can both begin and end with Job who, as Jung showed us, was able to grasp the antimony of God yet did not doubt His unity. Job called out for help from God against God, and thereby realized that God was at odds with himself. And that is the great realization which is hinted at in the various sources and is made quite explicit by Jung: the divine is a paradox which is both a union of opposites and thus conflictual, and is also unified into a blessed harmony. It remains for the human being to become aware that his own soul is "the dwelling place of God becoming conscious of Himself" and this is one function of Satan, the evil one. With this understanding of the problem of duality and unity, we can retrace our steps and both take up the various points wherein I promised further discussion, and also summarize the argument of the work.

At the outset, I stated that God both knew and did not know what He was doing when He told Adam and Eve not to eat of the fruit of the Tree of Knowledge. Now we can state that God's omniscience was fully aware of the consequences and even desired that event, since He needed a partner to share in His increasing consciousness of Himself. Yet He was ambivalent also, since He did not want humankind to "become as one of us." The answer, for me, is that this ambivalence is mirrored in the growth of each: Humankind must grow in consciousness and responsibility; we must become aware of how and to what extent we are immortal and "become as one of us," and how we are no more than the grains of sand, subject to this greatest sin of thinking of ourselves as "like unto God." God thus wants our consciousness and is aware that it is too much to ask, inflates us, is too much for us. With this gift from Satan, God's dark half, we share, finally, in the continuing evolution of consciousness.

This view is not in basic opposition to normative Judaism, since we know that the world is imperfect apart from God, that creation brought this evolution into being, and that the problem of duality—unconsciously that of God—is handed over to the human being. We are both one and many. We begin life with that pure wholeness that was like Adam's and Eve's; we continue with the realization of our division, as was also their experience; and we strive toward that re-integration of wholeness which is our task, our pain and our joy. In this, we, like Rabbi Akiba, transform creation.

The idea of conflict in God, as we noted from Kluger, makes sense, certainly, in our images of the divine. There is, of course, the *Ain Sof*, God as utterly Other, foreign and distant from us, but as creation and manifestation brings the divine itself to our experience—as we know from Kabbalah—the opposites are manifest, and, therefore, conflict takes place. This idea is highly congruent with Jewish mysticism. It makes sense, then, that the Divine needs both aspects of us: to grow in independence and choice, and to be connected and united with It. These needs are perforce in conflict at times.

We can also see that God wants humankind to see what He is really like and Job is our model. He accepts not only the good God, but the dark side as well. Thus he embraces divine conflict and, as Jung shows us, this brings about a tremendous transformation in religious development. This saw Christianity—the humanization of God—as the next step, and brings us to our own day, in which Jewish mysticism finds its parallel with the psychological findings. It is perhaps here that the God-man idea, so difficult for Jews, can be reconsidered in the light of psychology. We have the concept of the *Lamed Vovnikim,* for example, those righteous men who carry the burden of the divine in every generation. The psychological view is that we all can carry this image now, and thus the conflict of the God-man is latent in us all.

I wrote a story once in which the sequence of the suffering of those chosen by God went from the original 600,000 Jews said to be present with Moses at Mt. Sinai, reduced to the one God-man of the crucifixion, and that the suffering of 6,000,000 Jews of the Holocaust has carried us to a further step in development: we are all meant to be God-men and God-women, and to suffer the conflict of the divine opposites in ourselves. Those sanctified victims, a great number of whom were either children or fully observant followers of the Torah path, were, like Job, innocent. Perhaps the significance of their sacrifice lies in the fact that we are made poignantly aware of both the light and dark sides of the divine in the universe, in the world, and in ourselves.

In all this, we discover that God and man suffer from each other, so that the theme "ye are Gods" can be understood and realized. It is, thus, not God's purpose, apparently, to exempt man from conflict, hence the experience of evil, but to share in the divine conflict and, thus, in creation.

Now we come to Jung's observation that everything depends upon man's moral development, reaching a higher plane of consciousness, "in order to be equal to the superhuman powers which the fallen angels have laid in his hands." Are we up to this? Individually or collectively? I do not know. What we do know is that this task allies us with Luria's image of *Tikkun,* of unifying the name of God, of uniting male and female. For this we need *Kawwanah*, mystical intention, and *Devekuth*, mystical contact. Jungian psychology has shown us one way to do this; Jewish tradition has shown us another. Both agree that the Messiah can be found in each one of us. Perhaps if we all do our part, the expected Messiah will also emerge, not only from "within," but from "without" as well.

It is perhaps in this sense that we can understand the story that Urbach relates of the venerable Rabbi Joshua ben Levi, who said that the Messiah would come "today" if "you will hearken to his voice." I would understand this as implying that the redeemer, the Messiah, resides also in one's own soul, that if we but pay attention to this "incarnation"—namely the psychological realization that the image of God is a psychic content—then we can carry our share of the dialogue, the realization of the divine in our own lives. That realization is what gives significance to our existence. That is what Self-realization really means. We can also see it in its highest forms in the ecstatic and enlightened wisdom of such as Rabbi Akiba and Job, as well as in each person who has had his own glimpse of the divine antinomy and lived it.

REFERENCES

Berkovits, Eliezer (1965), *God, Man, and History*, Jonathan David, New York, 1965.

Fackenheim, Emil, (1986), "An Interview with Emil Fackenheim" by W. Novak, *New Traditions, Explorations in Judaism*, Summer 1986 No. 3, pp. 11-34.

Franz, Marie-Louse von (1974), *Shadow and Evil in Fairy Tales*, Spring Publications, Zurich.

Jung, C.G. (1958), *Answer to Job*, Collected Works, Vol. 11, Bollingen Foundation, New York.

Kluger, Rivkah Schaerf (1967), *Satan in the Old Testament*, Northwestern University Press, Evanston. Original 1948.

Meier, Levi (1981), *"Job, Judaism and Jung"*, Harvest, Journal for Jungian Studies, #27, pp. 7-13.

Moore, George Foote (1966), *Judaism in the First Centuries of the Christian Era. The Age of the Tannaim*, Harvard University Press, Cambridge, 3 vol.

Sholem, Gershom (1954), *Major Trends in Jewish Mysticism*, Schoken Books, New York.

Sholem, Gershom (1965), *On the Kabbalah and its Symbolism*, Routledge & Kegan Paul, London.

Urbach, Ephraim E. (1979), *The Sages; Their Concepts and Beliefs*, Magnes Press, Hebrew University, Jerusalem, 2 vols.

The Zohar (1936), translated by Sperling and Simon, Soncino Press, London, 5 vols.

PART III:
HARMONY AND DISHARMONY
TOGETHER

The following two stories, that of Julia the Atheist-Communist, and of the Medium, Sophie-Sarah, constitute a literary union of the harmony-disharmony discussed in the previous chapters. These two tales are to be found in my book, *The Tree: Tales in Psycho-Mythology*, (Phoenix House, Los Angeles, 1974 and Falcon Press, Arizona, 1982) which include stories or paths of individuation for ten different people, five men and five women, each of whom represents a different religious base, myth, or standpoint. They each have had a quest and all meet at the Tree of Life, discovering that their own symbols and stories are all part of that self-same tree. Julia and Sophie-Sarah are particularly Jewish stories, representing two different paths, but end up as part of world-including *minyan* of ten.

JULIA, THE ATHEIST-COMMUNIST

I.

My name is Julia. I have no idea how I came to this strange place; it is not my idea of Paradise at all. As a matter of fact, I am—or have been—an atheist for a good portion of my life. To me, Paradise has been a myth. I accept that this is where we are, though I cannot tell if I am in a dream or not. Perhaps you are all part of my dream—or even, that I am part of yours—I cannot tell.

I can say, however, that it is strange. You, Comrade Knight, look like something out of the Middle Ages. You, Arab, seem like a man of the eighteenth century. Or, if you are of my century, you are not like any Arab that I know, with your cattle and fences, but more like a cowboy! Ronin, since I know nothing of the Orient, I cannot tell from whence, in time, you come, but I would guess that you belong to the early nineteenth century.

I say all this, not because time matters to you—you would have said so if it did—but because it is important to me. You all seem somewhat timeless, eyes on the spirit and eternity. You do not even mention your names, as I do. You seem to be nameless, though I know better than that. Perhaps men are more impersonal than women are. All your differences are resolved in "The Quest" and, specifically, the quest for God or Union, or Enlightenment. You are ready to take all Eternity to find it. I don't know if that is particularly masculine, or because you all seem to belong to another age, but at any rate, it does not suit me.

I am clearly a child of the twentieth century. I feel myself to be very mortal, indeed, and am convinced that there is only one life—that into which we are born and suffer and die. I believe that it is our task to make the most of this life and to improve conditions on this dreary planet, for us and for our posterity. It is mankind that is to evolve and produce Paradise on Earth, not individual men, and not God.

Well enough. Let me tell you my story, since this seems to be what we are all here for. You will understand my views from it, rather than from my troubling to give you a lecture about it. I became disenchanted with lectures and polemics long ago.

I was born in 1926, in the common era, in a forested region in eastern Poland. There were only two houses in our little area, both belonging to members of our family—or, more accurately, to my Grandfather's families.

Each house was made up of children and grandchildren from his two marriages. Not that my grandfather was a bigamist—oh, no! He was a pious Jew who had managed to outlive his first wife. She died in childbirth with her tenth child. At the age of 72, the time of my birth, my grandfather was enjoying his full patriarchate, having sired 20 children and 40 grandchildren, of which I was the last.

I saw hardly anyone except the members of my family for the first seven years of my life. There was an occasional Polish peasant from whom we bought foodstuffs, or an itinerant peddler who brought us news from the world outside, but mostly the people I saw were brothers and sisters, aunts and uncles and cousins; some full, some half, but all happily mixed up together in a squabbling, loving impoverished way.

At the head of it all stood the proud figure of my grandfather. He was a giant of a man, for an eastern European, and he walked erect and firm with his seventy-odd years. When he sat at his large chair, he was awesome. How the family ever managed to get such an imposing chair, I don't know. It had a red damask seat and back, carved oak arms and legs—really a Spanish throne, in my memory. When grandfather sat in his chair, it was as if God were presiding over the fate of the world. Too much noise or chattering would distract him from the reading of his beloved Torah but he would show his displeasure with a roar and all would be silent. He returned then to his reading, puffing his pipe and stroking his long white beard. If my grandfather was not God, Himself, he was surely a direct descendant of Abraham, Isaac, and Jacob. We grandchildren called him *Zaideh*.

My grandfather was not a figure out of the Middle Ages, as you are, Comrade Knight. He came directly out of the Old Testament. I believe his psychology must have been like that of the pre-Christian era as well. yet I always enjoyed being with him, talking about the family history or about the woods which he seemed to know so well. Our family, he said, had been in the Polish forest for about three hundred years. We never owned the land, of course—how could Jews own land?—but there had been a tradition of leasing land, cutting the trees and selling the wood. Fortune had waxed and waned over the centuries: sometimes the family was wealthy, but usually there was barely enough to eke out a meager living. Since we always grew a few vegetables, and had a goat and chickens as did every Jewish family in forest or village in Poland, we managed to live reasonably well. We always had chicken on the Sabbath, for example.

Before coming to Poland, he said, his grandfather's grandfather's grandfather, back three hundred years, lived in Germany. There the family also worked in the forest and it was there, he thought, that they learned their trade. The sojourn in Germany had been brief, since they were expelled—in the typically sad history of the Jews—and came to Poland.

Before Germany, the family had been in Holland, where they were mirror-makers and lens-grinders. That much he knew for certain. There was a tradition that the family had previously been in Spain, my Grandfather explained, and had been expelled during the Inquisition. That seems likely in terms of my present knowledge of history and the movements of the Jews. Before Spain, North Africa, and before North Africa, Israel, which was left long, long before. Every year, at Passover, Grandfather would sit at the head of the table and, at the end of the *Seder*, shout, "Next year in Jerusalem!" How loud and joyous was his shout and our answering echo! Our life in the forest was good, nonetheless.

My grandfather loved me especially. I resembled him a little. My skin was fair, and my eyes blue like his, and my temperament was not unlike his. My hair, though, was different. I had dark, very curly, almost kinky hair, whereas he had straight red hair in his youth. His hair and my hair proved that we were hardly a "pure" family, racially. Clearly, Russian Cossacks and, very likely, African Negro, figured in the past history, and wanderings of our family since the destruction of the temple.

Not only did my grandfather love me, but my grandmother did too. If my grandfather were the archetype of the patriarch, my grandmother was the archetype of the matriarch and great Earth-Mother. She was big and buxom, clumsy and good-hearted, full of good humor, earthy wit and laughter. Sometimes she chattered too much and Zaideh would roar for silence. She was silent, but by no means afraid of him. "Bubeh," as we called her, had her own domain, and the Queen was just as royal as the great King. My grandmother loved me, as she loved all the children and grandchildren, by kissing us, patting us, blowing our noses, feeding us cookies, and protecting us from the wrath of offended patriarchal males. Her daughters were constantly berating her for her inefficiency, especially the daughters of the first marriage, but she took the criticism with good humor and ruled us all with love and warmth. Everybody loved her, despite their irritation with her.

My mother, her middle daughter, was her great champion. Mother was far more efficient and intelligent, though less able to be warm than Bubeh. My relationship to my mother was straightforward and matter-of-fact. We were probably very much alike in many ways. We seemed to have an unspoken understanding. She and I understood that we had to take care and be efficient, lest everything collapse; yet our love was such that we did not mind the other, inefficient females.

My father, however, was another matter altogether. He was a thin, silent man, with deepset and passionate eyes, always looking off into something else. He was rarely quite "there." It was not that he was a bit mad; no, not that. He was really something of a mystic, I think, though he was an ardent Communist consciously. My father had been a "catch." He had come from an educated family, and not only—as were the other males—in Hebrew and Talmud. He had been to the Polish schools and even had graduated from the *Gymnasium*, the High School. He could speak several languages and had a surprisingly romantic and violent past. Surprising, because when one looked at him, one saw a small and quiet man—not at all one for violence. He had seen a lot in his life, however. He had run prohibited Communist literature from Russia into Poland, tried to organize workers, led students, been in jail. His passionate nature had captured my mother, and his education was impressive to my grandfather, who deplored his politics and atheism.

Despite my father's hopes and aims to change the whole world, he was rather impractical, and could rarely manage to earn very much money. He would earn an occasional ruble as a translator, but he needed very little and was pleased to live in the kind of socialistic community of our little houses in the forest.

He was a decent father and took it upon himself to educate my brothers and myself whenever he was at home. When I was very little, he would tell me stories of all kinds that he would make up. I had only to give him a topic and off he would go into the wildest kind of fantasy. I loved it very much. I would especially ask for funny stories. These he found more difficult to create, but, seeing that I would grow hilarious and give a gross belly laugh like my grandmother to all of his attempts, he was encouraged to bring up whatever humor he could find. I was such an appreciative audience, I think, that he was amused by me in return. He was much harder on my brothers when it came to learning how to read, to write, to spell and to "do numbers." In fairness, he was also harder on me when I reached the age of five or so, when I began to perform the regular sets of lessons. I rarely gave him difficulty, unlike my brothers, so that his wild temper would seldom awaken itself in relation to me. When it did, I would cry and run from the room, which made him feel badly. I tried to restrain these little tantrums of mine for his sake, for I, just like my mother, absolutely adored this Great Man.

Now that I reflect on it, it is amazing that we had two Great Men in our household. Grandfather was, indeed, God; and God of the Fathers, of History, of the Torah, of the continuity of life both spiritual and material. For grandfather was also God of the Forest. He understood the plants and the trees and whatever little animals would manifest themselves in that place. He was also indomitable and conservative, orthodox and a benevolent despot.

My father, on the other hand, was the God of this World. He was for Change, for Humanity, for Life, for Liberty, for Progress, for making a New World. He was against the Capitalists, the Tyrants, the Exploiters, the Prejudiced, and so on.

Father and Grandfather respected each other and treated each other in a warm, though somewhat reserved manner. Each knew that the other had different views about life, politics, and especially about religion. Father was a confirmed atheist. They share goals, strangely enough. They wanted: for mankind, peace on earth and the brotherhood of man; for themselves, independence, good family life, friends, and the chance to pursue their intellectual interests.

My grandfather would say about Karl Marx: "A Jew who is not a Jew! Who ever heard of it! Paradise on Earth, yes, but without God? He has it all upside down! Too much *goyische* thinking in his head!" To which my father would answer, defensively: "All your religion, and all your Jewishness has brought the Jews nothing but pogroms, pain, and poverty! Where is your God at pogrom-time? No, we must make Paradise on earth, but *we*, Men must make it, and not wait for some Messiah to come on his white horse!"

That was the extent of their discussion when they got on the topic of communism or religion. They, neither of them, could really talk with the other on those topics, probably because both were so thoroughly committed to what they believed. Secretly, I think, each knew that the other had similar goals. Many times, when I was older, my father would say to me: "Don't tell him this, but I do believe that he is a greater communist than I! He is generous, wants the best for everyone, is ready to sacrifice for what he believes in, is a good and loving man." And my grandfather would say to me, on our occasional walks in the forest, "You know, your father is really a religious man. He wants all these things for men that God wants, and he is really religious in the right way: against hypocrisy, exploitation, and to bring Eden on Earth. God, anyway, loves atheists because they spend so much time thinking about him!" With that, he laughed, gave me a hug, and picked a flower for me.

Now that I think of it, these two men have been instrumental in my views, for I am fully and dedicatedly a Communist, though not nearly so naive and impractical a one as my father, and am an atheist like him. On the other hand, I believe in God, all right, but created in men's imaginations, out of their conditions of life. I know, like my grandfather, however, that a Jew must be a Jew. My view will become clearer later on. Right now I want to continue my story.

I could go on to describe my family: the lazy aunt who was a Communist, too, but only because she felt that whatever anyone else had was meant to be hers; the show-off cousin who always ruined our Passover feasts with her need for attention; a conceited cousin, smart and insufferable; the thieving uncle who stayed with us just for what he could get; yes, these unpleasant ones, and the many, many uncles, cousins, aunts, who were loving, generous, intelligent. And my brothers: those passionate, bright, difficult fellows who combined so much of father and grandfather. I weep as I think of them. I weep for them, dead, and I weep for myself, who has lost them, and I weep for the world, which has lost all the wonders that they would have brought to it. I cannot bring myself to say more about them right now. Maybe later, when I have brought you up to date about what happened to us all—maybe then, I will be able to tell you how good and generous and wise and wonderful they were.

Now, I can tell you that my childhood was happy and gay. I walked freely in the forest, alone or with my grandfather. I was safe with the birds and the little animals that would appear, and was always welcomed by the workmen, both family and others, who were busy cutting the trees. I loved to watch them at their work, pruning, paring, sometimes watering—for the forest was, in part, like a garden that they cultivated in order to produce a good crop. Part of the forest was wild and unattended. You know, it was something like this place. I would not have thought of it as Paradise—at least in my communist view of things—but I agree that my early childhood, my first seven years of life, was Paradise, indeed. Love, warmth, play, cheer, study, family, variety. Yes, a whole communist society and the forest, too.

When I was seven, however, a part of the family was compelled to move to the city. I was not clear about it at the time, but it seems that by 1933 an economic depression, originating in America, that golden land where everyone was rich, affected Poland deeply. It was now difficult to earn one's living. We could go on living on our own vegetables, but it grew harder and harder to sell the wood. The place would support only part of the family and the rest had to find sustenance elsewhere.

My father knew most about city life, so it was clearly our part of the family who would be the ones to leave the forest and try to make our way there. The great unity which had been in our family was giving way. Some of the people were Zionistic, and they wanted to stay in the forest until the time when they could emigrate to Israel. Others longed for opportunities in the promised land of America. Still others accepted things as they were and preferred to stay where they had always stayed.

It was easy, then, to decide. The Zionists and the Conservatives stayed in the forest with the grandparents. The Communists and the ones who wanted to improve their lot in America went to the city. We were about evenly divided, so nearly twenty of us went to the city to live. As I think of it now, our four groups: Religious, Zionist, Communist, "Americans"— demonstrated the forces affecting all Jewry at the time very well, indeed. I, myself, have been each of these, at one time or another.

So, many of us moved to the City. It was sad to leave the others, my grandparents, especially, but there was a certain adventure connected to going to the great City. Parting was made easier with the knowledge that we would visit Bubeh and Zaideh and the others when we could. So, just after my seventh birthday, a new phase of my life began.

II

If the first seven year of my life were those of the seven fat kine, the second seven were leaner. Paradise gave way to another reality, but it was not Hell. That infernal reality came to pass only during the last part of the second seven years.

It was exciting to come and live in the City, after our forest and country life. There were so many new things to see and hear. First of all, there were all the people, none of whom were relatives. On second thought, they weren't all that different—they were Jews after all! We lived in the Ghetto, in two rooms, just as crowded as we had been in the forest, but now the crowded conditions extended to our environment as well. In the forest, I could always take a walk and be utterly alone, if I wished. Now this was not possible. People were everywhere. The shops and dwellings were hard by each other, but the crowding gave warmth and I soon found a way to retreat into myself to be alone, rather than wander in the woods.

Besides the numbers of people and buildings instead of trees, what most struck me about the city was that the Jews seemed to walk bent, or in fear. Where was that pride that I saw in my grandfather when he walked in the forest? These other Jews did not have it—or rather, they only had it on Sabbath, when they walked to synagogue. What a sadness, that these men had dignity only in their worship and only on this one day, but not in their everyday lives!

When one left the Ghetto, it was like going into a foreign, hostile country. I did not understand this. In the woods, we all did pretty much what we wanted to do. There were rules and limits, of course, presided over by grandfather, father, and mother, but we felt free and safe. Now I felt neither free nor safe.

By the time I was ten or eleven, I better understood this sense of unease. First of all, my father was a Communist, making him suspect among not only the Poles, but the Jews as well. In addition to that, my father had taken on the age-old shrinking fear of the Jew in the alien and hostile land. It was an alien and hostile land, even though my family had lived there for three hundred years.

I became aware that the Poles were hostile to both Jews and foreigners when we went to school. It was made clear to us that going to school was a privilege which the Poles were only grudgingly granting us. Every day my two older brothers and I would walk to school safely enough, but coming home was often an agony. There would be cat calls, throwing of rocks, and shouts of "Jews" and "Christ-killers," especially at the times of our holidays or at Easter. My brothers were in continual fear of being beaten up.

They held their heads high, though they were quaking inside, and we hid all this from our parents. It was good that we did so, because they would have felt horrible about our situation, but powerless to remedy it. I was not the butt of jokes or pranks, but I suffered deeply for my brothers. It was not much better in the school. The teachers were brutal and often sadistic, especially when it came to the Jews. I had a first-hand experience of what I later learned was typical in our history: being forced to defend one's view when to do so is considered heretical and punishable with strict measures. It is like being called a witch when there are trials and witch-burnings—that is how it was to be a Jew in school in Poland in those days, as well as to be a Communist, later on, for me. In short, it is having to testify against oneself.

There had always been pogroms and anti-semitism in Poland, we knew, but the increasing intensity, apparently, was a consequence of the rise of the Nazi movement in Germany. We suffered, but somehow managed to keep our wits about us.

Life in the city grew worse and worse for me. The experience of anti-Semitism on the part of the Polish youth proved to be more painful than I first realized. It felt strange to be a foreigner in one's native land. But I cannot blame it all on the Poles. I also began feeling alienated from my fellow Jews in the Ghetto. I could not explain this, of course, in my early years, and even now I am at a loss to understand it altogether, but I do know that I steadily became more isolated and alone—more unhappy with the world as I found it and with myself.

As I grew older, I became conscious of myself more and more and did not like what I was beginning to see. I found that I was not pretty, though not ugly either. My hair, I despised, because of its kinkiness and my inability to do anything with it. I grew heavy and awkward, had thick legs and an ungainly walk—like a duck. I became increasingly closed, irritable, sensitive to the point of being touchy and withdrawn. My main solace was reading.

Thus I would be in the winter—withdrawn, neurotic, fat, unhappy, sensitive. In the summer, I would return to the forest, my Utopia. There were not only my grandparents, who made me feel beautiful and whole again, but also my cousins. We would play, dance, walk, talk. We would hike, swim, run, or sit quietly together. I was alone when I wished to be and had all the company I desired when I craved that. It was lovely. By mid-summer, I was always human again—thinner, healthier, tan and gay. Autumn and the return to the Ghetto would renew the pattern of withdrawal. It is hard to explain, though easy to describe. It was not that I was deprived of love, for my parents loved as best they could and this was more than substantial. Nor was it the lack of people about—for I could have had as many friends in the city as I had in the forest. I can only say, irrationally, that I was cut off from my own Utopia, the Forest, and that this was enough to make me ill, detached, and half-alive.

Life continued in this manner until my twelfth year. My father had been active in radical organizations, and I read more and more about such things. I was strongly attracted to the Utopian future of the Marxists, where each would receive what he needed and would give what he could, it all sounded like living in the forest with my grandparents and cousins. Besides that I was seriously religious, in an inner way, and could not accept the atheism. My father would talk to me about Communism, kindly and lovingly. His talk would shift to a glowing glimpse of the future. His vision was of the brotherhood of man, peace on earth—a Jewish vision, a Christian vision, and a Communist vision. For him, the atheist, unlike for Jews and Christians, God was excluded. I did not understand this. My religion was not very developed and differentiated, in truth, but I believed in God, all the same. I vaguely believed that God was located in the trees of my beloved forest. So I disagreed with Father.

In my twelfth year, as I have said, deep changes were beginning to take place. The ominous rumblings from Germany were growing louder and we lived in fear of what would happen to us if and when the Nazis should invade Poland. The Poles were bad enough, we knew, but the Nazis were even worse. In the midst of our worry and fear, my father grew ill.

We all have crucial life experiences which more or less mold us. These experiences, it is true, are not simply that one is molded and affected from outside, with no inner aptitude. That would be the naive environmentalism of those stupid Communists I subsequently knew and, I am ashamed to admit, like whom I also was for a time. I know that this outer experience also meets an inner core or aptitude, and that there is a basic, even historical, necessity in individuals and in the nation, for these events to occur. It is a strange magnetism, I think, of forces in interaction, and I do not in the least think of it as mystical. It is a kind of psychological-material synchronicity, a meaningful concatenation of inner and outer events from which none of us is free and most of us would wish to escape. We escape by fleeing either outward to the world, people, life, or inward to fantasy, dreams, thoughts. None of us really can escape, altogether. When these events occur, we know, even at the moment, that they are crucial for life. It was just such an experience when my father grew ill. His illness was no mystery. We knew what it was: cancer. It began in his throat and moved into his chest, and it grew with a rapidity which was astonishing.

The man had always smoked a lot. His intense eyes, and his hungers had always united in his manner of smoking cigarettes—which he consumed at a great rate. It was only in the Forest, when he did not—consume himself, I almost said—when he did not smoke at such a great rate. Yet I do not know if it was the cigarettes that had caused his cancer. My grandfather, after all, was an almost equally prolific smoker, though, it is true, he smoked and puffed on his pipe, rather than cigarettes. He did not, in short, inhale all the nicotine that my father did. Father's lungs, no doubt, were as black as they could be. Yet I do not believe that it was the cigarettes that cause my father's cancer. I think that it was the meaningful moment, the conjunction of events, inner and outer, which produced it. Father was consuming himself and was ready to die. That is what I think. His spirit and desire were more than his frame—thin and scholarly as it was—and the time—hellish and impossible as it was—could bear. So he consumed himself and died. I did not understand it this way at the time, of course. I saw only that Father was ill, suffering, pale. I saw the nearness of death for the first time in my life. We had already heard that Jews were not only displaced, beaten, put into camps in Germany, but were already dying for the crime of being Jews, and this was hard to believe. Now, whoever, death was much closer. Father was dying and we all knew it.

What could I do? I did what was deepest and best in me at the time: I prayed. I prayed to God to save this dear, compassionate, gentle man. I prayed to that great God of the Jews, who is open to human misery, who can change not only the course of history, but the course of individual life, the God who is passionately involved with His people. I prayed to this God. I prayed with the intensity and depth of my love, of my anguish, and even of my neurosis. Thus did I pray.

My father died. Yes, he died. I had asked God, I had promised God, I dare not tell you all the things that I had promised God I would do if only he would spare my father. It would only show you, as it does me, that I conceived even then that God could be bribed, cajoled, wanted sacrifices from men and would only then use his power beneficiently, but only perhaps. This was the God to whom I prayed. I prayed in vain. My father died.

At first, I had no feeling. I was numb. The funeral was as a dream to me in which I was merely a robot, not a dream with feeling or action or suspense or drama. I went though it and did not even weep. The daze lasted weeks. Mother cried, relatives cried, and Bubeh, dear Bubeh—she wept and held me and stroked me and looked for my tears, and she knew and wept some more. My sorrow was too deep for tears.

At last I went to Zaideh. He would know. I told him—dear Zaideh—of my prayer, of how I had asked God to spare my father and that he had not done this. My grandfather sat quietly. He was silent a long time. He then spoke with a cool and timeless depth. His words were brutal. He spoke in Yiddish, and in a way that I cannot translate. He reminded me first of years before, of the stories that I had been told about the first World War, of how my father had to go to war and was in danger of losing his life, and of how my grandfather's sons were also called up, and had to serve in the hated army of the hated Poles. My grandmother had wept and moaned, Grandfather reminded me, and he had said, "If they have to go, hey have to go; if they are wounded, so they are wounded; and, if they die, so they die." He reminded me of this story, which I had heard a hundred times. Each time I heard it before, it was as if the different characters of the two people, Grandmother and Grandfather, were being extolled and cherished: Grandmother weeping and in agony, Grandfather cool and detached for all eternity. The archetypes lived and one heard them. Besides, no one died, so it could be merely an entertaining story. Now the genuine event occurred, and I saw the eternity of my Grandfather. I saw his coolness and I was astonished.

I looked into Grandfather's eyes. I looked deeper into these eyes of the same blue color as mine but vast and bottomless. I saw into them and that which I saw changed everything. The words and the demeanor said one thing, the eyes another. In the midst of those eyes were suffering and anguish, the enduring of pain that I have rarely seen before or since. Those eyes revealed the suffering of the Jews and of all people, from time eternal. They showed the suffering of the one who knew he was in the hands of God, and that God's ways were different from man's. My grandfather was Abraham, and Isaac, and Jacob, all in one; more than that, he was Job. I loved him, and I loved his suffering.

But something cracked inside me. An illusion, a faith, a belief was broken. All I knew was that God was dead. I denied Him. It was then that I became an atheist. That, as you will see, is the central fact of my story, though I will tell you many other things. You will see in my story what this all means. But there, before my thirteenth birthday, I lost faith in God.

III

The next months are somewhat vague in my mind. My father's death catalyzed the family into action. It was expected that war would soon come and the specter of the Nazis was very great for all of us. We knew that we had to leave the country, but this was impossible, since there was no money for that. Failing that, the old, the feeble and the young had to leave. We had been receiving frantic letters from some distant relatives in America, who were, like us, terrified of the Nazis and wanted desperately for all of us to come to the Golden Land of America. There was enough money, at this time, for only a few. After full family discussion, it was decided that my grandparents, my mother, and myself should take the tickets and come to America. My brothers and the others would somehow take care of themselves for a time, until more money would be forthcoming. There was much protest about this arrangement—from my grandfather who wanted to stay in the land of his ancestors, and from my grandmother, who hated to leave any part of the brood unattended. My grandfather was convinced to leave when he was reminded that he always hated the Poles anyway, that the land was never his nor his ancestors, but was always leased, that the true promised land was Israel, to which we might all go one day, but that we were poor and had to earn some money first. Grandfather listened to all of this, needed the guarantee that there were plenty of orthodox Jews in America, and then agreed to go. Grandmother was reassured that soon the rest of the brood would be brought over and was given a solemn promise of this by my mother—something that she was to bring up again and again when the awful truths were later known. I am getting ahead of my story. At this point, it was agreed that Bubeh, Zaideh, my mother and I should go.

Once this was decided, and the money for tickets and visas received, we quickly set out for Danzig. We were full of excitement about going to America. I can still remember the ferment of the port, and of the people. Just the other night, I dreamed about it once again and saw it as clearly as I see you all right now. The Summer of 1939, the people in their caps, shawls, starched clothes. The atmosphere of fear, even panic. The feeling that the world might be coming to an end. The anguish on the faces of the Jews, especially. The Poles seemed less aware, and only an occasional face had real fear in it. My family had our own blend of fear, excitement, hope, and sadness at leaving our loved ones and our beloved Forest. It was then that I was able to put aside my grief at the death of my father. The vision of the pain in my grandfather's eyes, earlier, had enabled me to weep, and weep I did, copiously, for days. My grandfather comforted me, my mother comforted me, but my grandmother comforted me the best—she wept with me! Oh, did we weep! We wept together for days until, at last, we were wept out. My mother's grief was greater than our own, no doubt, but she did not have the gift of letting her emotions go, and thus she contained it all. I suppose she felt the need to be strong, take care of us. She must have known, even then, that not only was her husband dead, but that her family would be separated and that she might never see her sons again. Now that I think of it, she was the bravest woman that I ever saw. I do not believe that I could endure this myself.

But now, at the ship in Danzig, I could let my grief rest and I could think of a new life, a new beginning in America, the Golden Land. As it is with the young, hope and new life are powerful and take precedence over death and separation. I had now passed my thirteenth birthday, and, although I was not a boy and subject to Bar Mitzvah, everybody knew that girls matured more quickly than boys, and if boys become men at thirteen, I was surely about to become a woman.

We had hardly arrived in America, in noisy, frightening New York, when war broke out. I remember the day very well, because it was the day that I had my first menstrual period, September 1, 1939. I was 13, becoming a woman, the war broke out and I bled. My mother was lovely. She had warned me beforehand, so I was prepared, but I was awkward and embarrassed, nonetheless. When she gently slapped my face on both sides and said words like "put-put, Mazeltov" I laughed. It was a ritual and it meant I was a woman. She laughed, too. She did not know what it meant, but knew that her mother had done that to her and so she did that to me. Mother then called my grandmother into the bathroom, to tell her the great news, and my grandmother promptly performed the same ritual. Then we all sat down and laughed uproariously, almost forgetting that I needed care. It was a lovely experience, I think, one which helped spare my neurosis from attaching itself to being a woman. With all my *mishigas*, as they say, my fundamental being as woman has never been questioned or hurt, thank goodness.

All the same, it is interesting that the day that Poland was invaded by Germany, the day World War II officially broke out, the day that began the Holocaust for the Jews, that was the day that I bled and became a woman. There had been a meaningful correspondence between the death of my father and the death of God. Now there was a meaningful correspondence between the death of the Jews and my bleeding and becoming a woman. The profundity of this is beyond me, but, despite my rationality, I accept the meaningfulness of the symbol, with all its ambiguity, without question.

We listened carefully to the news each day after that, wondering about the fate of my brothers and the rest of my family. Our relative in New York was far from rich, so again we were crowded into his two room flat, along with his wife and young children. They were kind to us, and we were all glad to share our common fate as Jews, but it was also clear that we soon would have to fend for ourselves. At this point, we were glad to have any shelter at all and could laugh because things were just like the Old Country, in this, the land where streets were paved with gold, except that now the animal which lived with us was not a goat, but a cat!

We could tell nothing about our family from the news of the war, but we felt better that France and England were going to fight. Surely they, civilized people that they were, would defeat the Germans, and we would soon be re-united with our family.

Our mood was tense, but hopeful, and Mother started making arrangements for us to go to California, where she had already been promised work as a translator and as an advisor in the film industry. This sounded very glamorous and I thought that America might be a Golden Land after all!

Living in Los Angeles proved to be immediately pleasant and easy for us. Mother got the job that was promised and her pay was very good. Indeed, I am not sure of the amount, but she often said that she was earning more than the combined income of all the families of our two houses in the Forest, plus half the Jews of the Ghetto in the city. She remarked about how many Jews there were in Hollywood, how vulgar they were, but how nice and considerate all the same. Many were rough in speech and ill-tutored, for a Jew anyway, but underneath, she said, they were generous and loving. I did not know anything about that. All that I knew was that soon we had a warm and friendly home in the Hollywood Hills, that I had my own room to myself, that all sorts of interesting people were coming to our house, that my grandparents were content in the new place, and that Mother was making a new life for herself.

We now had security, warmth, and a good life. There were many trees again and lots of good places to walk in the hills, even if it was not the Forest. Despite our good fortune, I was still quite unhappy with myself.

My kinky hair grew worse. My piano legs and duck walk made me more self-conscious than ever and I seemed to be unable to do anything about either. I was quite aware of boys, but terrified lest any of them approach me. If only my brothers had been there, I thought, they would pave the way. That was where we all were most unhappy: we missed my brothers.

The news from Europe grew more and more ominous: Poland defeated, France and the Low Countries invaded and defeated, as well. Only England survived and with little chance of eventual triumph. America was supportive but afraid, or inept, or isolationist.

Worst of all, Russia had deceived us. My father had been Communist, it is true, but of the Trotskyite persuasion. Though he continually hoped for the World Revolution, for the triumph of the World Communist State, he did not have much regard for Stalin. All the same, we still had great hopes for the first Communist state—even those of the family, the majority, who were not Communist. There was expectation that something new would emerge out of such an experiment. When the Russians invaded Finland, we were greatly disappointed, but rationalized that they had to defend themselves against the Fascist base near their chief city, Leningrad. When they invaded Poland, we were shocked, especially since they had made a pact with Hitler. This we could not rationalize so readily, but still, we could not believe that a Communist would be so bad as a Nazi. I still read avidly in the Communist literature and was deeply impressed with all the Russians had accomplished. I loved the Russian films. Despite all evidence to the contrary, I was sure that the negative things could be explained, were just capitalist propaganda or were temporary expedients in the face of threat.

More horrible for us were the reports of the concentration camps in Germany and elsewhere. The Jews were being destroyed, it was said. We could not believe it. When Russia was invaded, we were glad, for now the "good people"—Communists and western democracies—were united against the common foe. In time, our people would be free. Thus the years went, until America was in the war. It is a history known to all—at least all who lived at the time. That history is not what I wanted to tell you about in my story. What I want to relate is what happened to my soul. I wish to reveal the inner story of my life, as well as the outer events.

These crucial events began to occur after the war was over. When victory was achieved, we finally learned the fate of our fellow Jews: six million dead. When my grandmother realized the full extent of what happened—the death of sons, daughters, grandchildren—she went mad. At first she moaned and groaned and complained, asked questions, and blamed everyone for not bringing the others with us. All attempts to reason with her were impossible. She let herself go altogether, fell back into a shell and simply died. It all happened so fast that it was hard for us to realize it. She was quite old at the time, over 75, but like all the peasant types of my family, there was every reason to believe that she would go on living in good health until 100. She simply died, however, and her death had a certain rightness about it. She was relieved of her suffering, at least.

In caring for Bubeh, mother hardly had a chance to grieve for herself and, when she did, she did so privately. It was as if she, too, had cut herself off, as if the loss of the sons was too much to bear.

I moved toward my grandfather, who sat silently in his chair, puffing on his pipe. He had been silent all through the later years—reading his Yiddish newspaper, taking his daily walk, saying his prayers, going to the synagogue. Now he was more silent than ever. The deaths of all the Jews went into him to the marrow, but he said nothing. The deaths of our personal family members seemed only a part of the larger whole. When my grandmother died, he took this in, he absorbed it in the same timeless way.

I went to Zaideh to speak to him. I wanted to ask him how it was that his God, whom I had given up at the death of my father years before, had allowed this to happen. When I came to him, however, I dared not speak to him thus. Why should I be so cruel as to push my atheism upon him? I loved my Zaideh. After my father, there was no other man who was so fine and upright and decent. So I went to him to comfort him. I went to Zaideh, not for answers, not for help and solace, but as a loving granddaughter. I went with love and warmth, with tears in my eyes for his suffering. When I went thusly to this great old wise man, this silent rock, this Job, this Moses, this Abraham, Isaac and Jacob, this patriarch who was the same as all the Jewish patriarchs who ever lived—this man took me in his arms and wept. He wept and sobbed and held me to him; he said not a word, but cried and I cried too. It was not the end of the world that this man, who was, for us little children, the representative of God on earth, could not answer us, for he, too, was human.

We wept, and then my mother came, and she wept, too. We cried, together, the three of us. For days was it? For weeks? Or was it just minutes or hours? I do not know. We held each other closely and wept for what it was to be a Jew, and Human Being. The strange thing is that my grandfather's faith was not shaken. When I later asked him about this, why he did not give up his faith in God with such horrible events, he answered simply that it was not a question of his choice, for God had already chosen. He, Grandfather, was chosen, all Jews are chosen, and one could neither get out of it, nor change it. One could only pray to God to release us from His wrath and to bring us under His wing of love.

I was touched by my grandfather's faith and his endurance, but I was still an atheist and a Communist, though in a way different than before. I could not formulate it then, for that had to wait until later, but that night I had a dream.

In my dream, I was down low, under the earth, being oppressed by the burden and pressure of earth all around me. I pushed my way up to the surface, where I was free again and could breathe. Here I caught a glimpse of my family, but just a glimpse of them, waving happily at me. Now I wanted to go toward them, but I felt a pressure, another pull, driving me up, up off the ground. I tried to work against this pull upwards, just as I had tried to overcome the pressure downwards before. I tried to hold onto the ground and the trees, but the pull dragged me up into the air. I was frightened and angry at being pulled away from my family, but the force would not be denied. As I ascended, I was told or I knew—I am not clear which—that I was being brought to the presence of God. Now I was more frightened and angrier. I was unbelieving and thinking this a trick. Then I changed; in the dream, I changed: I decided to bring my complaint to God. I decided that I would rise up to God and complain to Him about how He treated Man, how terrible He had been to His Chosen People, and how He was not entitled to be worshipped and prayed to by the people and how I no longer believed in Him, anyway.

With this infusion of anger, of questions, firmness and rage, I heard a Voice. It said: "She speaks truly of the Lord, listen to her." I found myself sinking back to the earth, gently, easily, until I found myself safely resting in my bed.

This dream made a great impression upon me. I came to a peace which I had never known before. I also came to a firmness that I had not felt. It was as if my anger and my questions and my atheism—especially my atheism—were being sanctioned and encouraged by God! What was that? That God affirmed my atheism? I did not understand this fully at the time, but this has been the chief paradox of my life: my atheism is God-given, and I worship the Highest in that. So I do believe at this moment. Much else happened in my development later on—of which you will shortly hear—but this paradox has stayed with me. I rose up to God and complained to God, and rejected God for his unwonted cruelty to Man and to his Chosen People. I aver that I am an atheist and that God has agreed with me, and has told me that I speak truly of God.

So, now, my friends, so it was that the third seven-year cycle of my life came to an end. With the first, I came out of the Paradise of the Forest into the City; with the second, I rejected God upon the death of my father; with the third, God affirmed my rejection of Him, and embraced my vision as true. I discovered paradox, and came into my own search, which is why, probably, that I am fortunate enough to find myself among you able and illustrious people in this place of the origin of us all, Paradise.

IV

In 1946, before my 21st birthday, I decided to leave America for Israel. The dream had been decisive in my development. It had said nothing about how I was to live my outer life, but, all the same, I knew that I had to do this. I was an atheist in a special sense, and I was deeply aware of this, but I was also a Communist, though not as yet in a special sense. I knew that I could not stand my fellow Communists, most of whom were simply greedy, power-hungry, domineering little people. I was also glad that I had never joined any organization so as to get myself into trouble with Communist-hunters. I knew, however, that I was a Communist, just as my father had been, but I did not know in what way I was meant to be one.

I was now more Zionistic than ever and felt that whatever my fate as a Jew and as a Communist was, that I would spend it in Israel. As soon, therefore, as my studies were completed at the University, I saved my money and made ready for my trip to the Holy Land. By this time, my mother was well ensconced in her work in Hollywood and had met a man of whom she was deeply fond. He, too, had lost his spouse, was lonely, and wanted to marry her. It seemed right for Mother to embark on a new life, just as I was ready to go abroad and be fully on my own. It felt natural that grandfather should come with me to Israel to live, while Mother would continue her life in America. Thus it came to pass.

<h2 style="text-align:center">V</h2>

In the Fall of 1946, I completed the third seven-year cycle of my life and went to Israel with my grandfather. Zaideh had now spent as many years in the twentieth century as he had in the nineteenth, but he was almost as strong as ever. We both knew, however, that at ninety-two, he was going to Israel to die. He was doing this for the whole line of our family, for those who had come out of his loins and had been burned in the ovens.

It was a great and meaningful voyage. We went slowly—on a ship, and it was a Jewish ship. My grandfather marveled that here was a ship both owned and run by Jews. We wondered how we would be in that Jewish land.

We knew how we would be—happy! When we arrived, the land spoke. It said, "Welcome, Oh Jews! Shalom! Welcome to you, for you come Home, at last." And it was a homecoming! We kissed the land and felt its dry warmth. The trees and the stones spoke to us, and everywhere we went, we rejoiced at the names of the places—places which had names in the Bible and in history, but had—almost—been forgotten as realities. My grandfather was so joyous in Jerusalem, he danced. Oh, how he danced at the synagogue of the Chasidim! He danced and he prayed. In truth, he had never been a formal member of the Chasidim—he had been a traditional Jew—but he had read, he had studied, he had watched, and he had talked. Now, now that he was in Jerusalem, of whom it was written, "If I forget thee...", he was in the place of his soul. He danced and he wept, and he was home.

He was, indeed, at home in the Meah Shearim of Jerusalem, the old city of Jews living, really, in the middle ages. He was at home, but I was not. After a time, when I found that he would be happy and taken care of, I left him there and went to live at a Kibbutz in the Gallil, which was as communistic as one could desire.

During the years in Los Angeles, I spent summers in a Zionist camp, where I had been quite happy. It was, indeed, a repetition of the pattern I already knew in Europe: winters of neurosis, introversion, unhappiness, study; summers of outdoor life, walking, being with family or alone in the forest, happy. It continued in Southern California, only now it was summer camp, rather than forest. Now, in Galilee, I was in a perpetual summer camp in the forest, along with a new "family"—all my fellow Kibbutz members. It was a if the remnants of my neurosis fell away, for I was at one with everyone in work and play and study. Work, comradeship, dancing, community. It was lovely. It was my nature to be extraverted and now, at last, I was on my own soil and living my own life.

It seemed that I was back in Paradise. Shortly after my arrival, there also arrived a handsome young American who was also Zionistic and who looked upon me with a fire in his eyes—what more could I ask? Now, in my fourth cycle of seven, Paradise had returned. The young American and I were married, and it was a source of great joy in the Kibbutz. We danced all night. Even my grandfather, whom we brought from Jerusalem, now became reconciled to all the pain and evil in his life. He knew that our family line could continue. I would surely give birth to a son.

Life was good. In 1948, the War of Independence came and we fought for our lives. That war is well known. Needless to say, we gave everything we had, and the celebration of our own land, of proclaiming the Jewish State after two thousand years—this was almost too great a moment in history. The war was hard, all the Arab states united against us, but we won and the land was ours.

We went back to our labor and our life, to build our Jewish State and to welcome back from the Diaspora all the Jews who were now clamoring to come. It was miraculous and the flood of emotion made me almost forget that my special "Chosenness" was atheism. I had to reflect upon what my communism would be. I had seen too much and known too much to be the naive Communist that my father had been—the Trotskyite believing that all men would soon be brothers, the workers of all the world would soon overthrow their rulers. I had seen too much for that and knew that the era of nationhood, of states, still had a long way to go. I knew that the Jews, above all, had to have their own State for a very long time. I also knew that what the Russians had done, their abridgment of freedom, would not be tolerated as communism, and that Marx, too, had turned everything upside down. What kind of a Communist was I? Hardly one at all. Yet, I was.

After a few years of routine, of work and the regularity of life in our Kibbutz, I began to have periods of depression, without knowing what it was all about. I no longer felt joyous in my work, which was to care for chickens and sort the eggs, nor did I feel happy when I awakened in the morning. I loved my husband, there was no doubt of that. He seemed intent upon his own activities and very busy. He not only did his daily task—which was to care for the trees in the orchards—but in his spare time he continued to work on his dissertation for his doctoral degree.

What was it that I was experiencing? Was it a further disillusionment with the Communist way of life? Was it a breakdown of the meaningfulness of life? I did not know. When I tried to communicate these feelings to my husband, he was sympathetic, but he did not really seem to understand, nor to connect with what I felt. I suppose that I did not convey to him the depths of my despair. How could I? It seemed too absurd to speak about depression and despair when I answered every question with a statement of satisfaction. Did I love my husband? Yes. Was I happy to be married? Yes. Did I feel that I was doing a meaningful work in the Kibbutz? Yes. Did I like it? No, not any more, but I did not despise it either. Was I glad to be living in Israel? Yes, indeed. Did I feel patriotic and believe that I was living in an important time in history? Yes, a man's question, indeed, not a woman's, but I felt that it was important. So, all questions that would be asked of me, I could answer either affirmatively or in a way that could not account for my recurring times of lassuetude, depression, crying spells.

There was only one place in my life that seemed to have a connection with my state: I was not getting pregnant. For the first few years of our married life, my husband and I were pleased not to be having children—we wanted to know and experience each other first, before the distraction of a family. It was not that children would be a burden, financial or emotional, in our lives. Not that; for the Kibbutz was organized on communistic lines. Though the babies stayed with their parents evenings, they lived largely in a nursery with other babies and children, and were cared for by nurses and teachers. Parents would be with their children in their free time and when both wished, but there were no family house units, as such. We were not fearful of the responsibility since the whole community took care of that. We just wanted to have no other people to distract us from our emotional connection with each other

After a few years, however, we no longer felt this way, and were ready to have children. We wanted a boy and a girl, at least, and were looking forward to that pleasure. I also felt that it was important to my grandfather that I have a son, for his sake, and that the strong, healthy line that came out of him, so destroyed by the Holocaust in Europe, would continue with me, his granddaughter. My husband and I even agreed that if there were a son, we would give him, as a middle name, the surname of my grandfather's family. When we told Zaideh our plan, this gave him great pleasure and, as they say in Yiddish, *naches*. It was as if this would be the final crown to my grandfather's long life and make it possible for him to die happily, despite the enormous tragedies.

Yet we were not having children. At first, we thought that it was just a question of time, and that the children would soon come, I, after all, came from a highly prolific family, and my husband did also. We went to be examined. It appeared that there was nothing physically preventing conception, from either side, and our respective contribution to having children—sperm and egg—were both quite normally viable. Whey we were not having children was not known and, therefore, "psychological."

At first, I rejected psychological explanations as being no explanations at all. It was just another way of saying that the reasons for our not having children were not biological. My husband would make little jokes in the English language, saying such things as "my wife is impregnable, no...unbearable...no, inconceivable."

I was rather annoyed with these jokes, but realized that he, too, was pained and that his jokes were merely regressions to his American sense of humor, which was not very deep. I realized, too, that my own reaction was to fall back to my Polish-Jewish touchiness and paranoidal feeling of being demeaned. Finally, we both wept together in each other's arms, and admitted that we were desolate about it. Our sorrow did have the effect of bringing us closer together for a time. Now, at last, I had an outer situation and event to which to attach all my despair and unhappiness, but I knew in my heart of hearts that my inability to have children at this time was not the only reason for my despair.

It was 1953. My husband received his doctoral degree the year before. I was twenty-seven years old and my grandfather was now—praise God, I would say if I were not an atheist—ninety-nine years old. For some time, my husband had been speaking about going to Switzerland to study postdoctorally to become a qualified psychotherapist. It had been his desire for a long time, but it seemed to be difficult to find the funds to do so. I, too, looked forward to a change—in truth, I missed Europe, and its green. Even though our Kibbutz was in the north of Israel, and there was forest, I knew from my childhood how the rain-swept forests of Europe can be, and I missed them. I thought that perhaps I, too, could be analyzed and find the cause of my barrenness. For now, in my heart of hearts, I was beginning to believe that my inability to have children was of a psychological origin beyond my conscious awareness. I had read in psychology and felt new vistas open up to me, but was still, as a communist, something of a doubter and scoffer.

When my husband received a grant from an international association to study in Switzerland, however, and the Kibbutz placed no objection to our going, we were both overjoyed. In 1953, the fourth seven-year cycle of my life was coming to an end, and the fifth one was to begin. I began to feel meaning and pattern in my life again—not that I understood it. Rather I felt that with the move, the meaning might emerge.

All that remained was to see my aged grandfather, who was very weak and living in a home of Elders in his beloved Meah Shearim in Jerusalem. I visited him a month before our scheduled departure, knowing that this would be the last time that I would see him alive. I talked to my Zaideh, no longer spry, nearly blind, quite weak, though apparently aware enough to be sensitive to my need to see him and make it right with him before I left.

"Oh, little Julia," he said, patting my head. "I know why you come now, before you move again from our land, to pursue your husband's career and your own need. I know, little one. I know that you will miss me, and that we will not see each other again. I know that you come in sadness, for not giving me a grandson and a granddaughter who will continue my line and my tree. Please, do not grieve for this, for it is a sign from God. I do not believe it to be a punishment...no...I believe that you, like me, and like all of us Jews, are chosen. You, dear Julia, are chosen in a way that neither I, nor even you, as yet, can fathom. I am ninety-nine years old and I have been chosen by God to live long and watch the destruction of great numbers of my people, to see the death of my parents, and my brother and sisters, and my wives, and all my seed but one, and why the Lord has given this unto me is a great mystery. But the Lord has also, in this same era and in this same time, given my people back its land—that for which we longed for two thousand years, and He has brought me here to live in it, and to worship Him, my God, in His Holiest of Cities. This, too, He has done. The Lord giveth and the Lord taketh away, and He giveth again, and mysterious are the ways of the Lord... You, little Julia, are like Sarah, to me, of old, and of our father Abraham. For she, too, was barren, and she was the ancestress of our line. Do not tell me, Julia, that I am wrong, that I put too much on you, that you are far from Sarah, but just an ordinary Jewish girl. That may be so, but I feel you to be otherwise, and that you are the end and the beginning of a new era for the Jews. Perhaps not you alone—I do not burden you with that, but leave it to God. You, like Sarah, are burdened and barren. God will come to you, and make you fecund and creative and of a new line, and you will feel—as did Sarah—the breath of God in your name, the Ruach Elohim. That breath will make you fertile, and a new line from which I come will be continued. Such is it that comes to me, and blessed be thee, my sweet Julia, the last of my seed."

Zaideh put his hand on my head and then turned his face to the wall. I knew that a patriarch of old had spoken to me and I trembled in awe. It was my beloved Zaideh, the ordinary man that I had known all my life, but, at the same time, he was Abraham, and Isaac and Jacob, and the last of the Patriarchs. God had spoken to him and given me a message. I was shaking and crying and at peace—all at the same time. It was as if, at last, the deep darkness in my soul, with which I had lived with for several years and which had come up as a wordless despair, was now being reached by this old man's words. He was connecting with the dark, abysmal place and making it meaningful. He was not giving an answer, but he was, as the Quakers say, "speaking to my condition" and my being was responding to him.

After a long time, when I could recover myself and speak to Zaideh, I spoke again. But he was asleep. He seemed to be smiling in his sleep, as if joyously beholding the vision of a happy place, or an answer to his soul's desire, and I did not wish to awaken him. I went out of the room and went to my own room to sleep the night and rest from that encounter. That night I had the first dreamless, peaceful sleep that I had had in a long time. I awakened refreshed and ready for the new phase of my life. When I went to bid good-bye to Zaideh, I was not surprised to be told by his nurse that he had died peacefully in his sleep during the night. Zaideh had forgiven me my barrenness—nay, he had promised great things from it, and now he could die, with the assurance in his own soul that his life was not in vain and that I would continue his seed. Praised be the Lord of my grandfather, for making him happy. But let it be acknowledged that I was following my own path of being the atheist, for thus was I chosen.

We buried my grandfather in the land that he had finally attained and with him we buried a long and wonderful and painful history. The day was beautiful—the sky clear, but unusually cool. People came from everywhere for the funeral of my grandfather—it was a great event. Mother came from America, and it was as if all the Jews of the Meah Shearim were there to celebrate him. There were tears, it is true, but there was joy and a feeling of peace—for my grandfather had come home to Israel and to his God and all was well.

In the Fall of 1953, well after my twenty-seventh birthday, my husband and I took up residence in Switzerland, in the city of the "Great Psychologist," to study at the Institute which bore his name. How can I convey the feelings and impressions that I had upon my arrival? Before we arrived, on the slow Dutch freighter that we had taken from Haifa to Genoa, and on the train from Genoa to Zurich, I had many thoughts and impressions. I had summarized the first seven years of my life as in the primordial paradise. The second seven years took me from this Eden into a gradually worsening purgatory to a horrible hell at the end. The third seven-year cycle found me in a gradually improving purgatory in America and again finding paradise in Israel during the fourth seven-year period. This time, however, during the last half of the fourth cycle, I had a kind of paradise outside with an unknown and increasingly hellish purgatory within. Now I was arriving in a "psychological holy place"—as distinct from a religious one—which, hopefully, would help me mend or bring together these heavens and hells into a livable unity. Or, at least, give me some explanation for it all. What was psychology for, after all? My husband had no such deep problem at the time. He was there simply to be trained better, to be educated better, and to do his proper work in the world.

If he had any deep inner problems, they were not apparent to either him or me, and he was just glad to be in Switzerland, finally studying in the place he had long desired to be.

Our arrival already set the atmosphere. We emerged out of the train station in the late afternoon on a rainy, dreary day into a wonderful old European city. I immediately felt something stir in me. I could not formulate it then, but now I can see it as a coming into life again of a whole period of my soul. If Israel represented the ancient and deepest layer of the human part of my psyche, as well as the most modern and recent part, then America represented the generally modern part, but Europe was everything in between. Europe was from 70 C.E. to the nineteenth century. America was the nineteenth century and into the twentieth, but surely Europe was everything in between. In a way, this represented my own life as well. My grandfather represented Israel and the whole dim past, where I was raised in a forest, similar to these beautiful forests that I had seen on the train coming into Switzerland, and these buildings, these old buildings looked rather like those in Poland, too. I was going to live again in the continent of my birth.

We were quickly settled in our little apartment and taken by friends up an old cobble-stone street to acquaintances of theirs. There we sat, in a fine, old, quiet living room, with an ancient tile stove, in the midst of Swiss cleanliness, positively burgher-like comfort and security, looking out of the window to the great lake of the city. We sat there quietly, nibbling cheese and drinking wine. How can I tell you what I felt? It is in the heart to say: I wept inwardly with great joy and felt that I had come home.

That is a strange thing to say, isn't it? For a Jew, for one who was born in a Polish forest, for one who lived long in America, for one who also felt that she had come home when she went to live in Israel—all of that is an unexpected background for one who feels she has come home in the rainy, quiet atmosphere of Switzerland! It was so. I could not explain it then, but now I understand it somewhat as follows: Israel represented my spiritual home, the home of ancestors and the spiritual meaning of my life. Switzerland, however, was a home for my soul, the womb-like place where one could be safe, go into one's self, be well-fed and clothed and warmed, attended to and educated from within. Israel was the home of the Fathers, Switzerland the home of the Mothers. I wonder if others see it that way, too. Or is it only me? Virgo, the Jungfrau, after all, is an astrological symbol for Switzerland, so it makes sense to see it as feminine. That others may not see it that way might be because the Swiss women are not notably attractive compared to Italian or Greek or Spanish or French women. There are many pretty Swiss girls, but I think, too, of those dried-up, thin-lipped ones who are terribly tight and constantly cleaning their floors! I stand firm, however, in thinking that the beautiful Swiss landscape, its care for beauty, comfort, positive order, is, indeed, a good mother. I do not insist that you see it that way. That is just how I experienced it.

I was very happy that first evening, enjoying the wine and cheese, looking over the beauty of that remarkable lake and city.

My husband and I settled into the life of the city, as students and foreigners. It was perfect, for the Swiss know how to treat both—leave them alone as far as possible, as long as they do not disturb life. The Institute was ideal, for it was filled with people from all over the world, old and young, many coming to study to become psychotherapists, or simply to continue their own development.

There were quaint old ladies from England and America, whom my husband at first deplored—they were so unprofessional and unbecoming to his desired image of the proper psychotherapist—but I rather liked them. Later on, even he admitted that they often knew a great deal more about psychology than he did, and finally he liked them as much as I did, and came over to the view that it would be terrible were this to be just another professional institute with so many dull, deadly serious young men and women out to improve their role and income. Praised be the old ladies, the young strange men, and all who made that place into the unique and alive place it was.

There were many teachers and speakers. There were the regular faculty, who had spent long years with the Master, and the visitors from all over Europe and, indeed, from other parts of the world. Even from Israel, I was glad to see. They lectured on mythology, religion, psychopathology, and all manner of related things.

The main thing was one's own analysis. That was it. One was "in a process" and that was a secret, private thing, that people did not discuss with each other very much. They could talk about deep matters, and about theory, and people, and all the usual things, but they didn't talk much about their analytic work. I liked that a lot and, from being a scoffer about psychology, I became pleased and positive and a booster. It was not long before I was "in analysis" as they said, myself. I had planned to do so, of course, for I had to find out about this deep, dark place in my soul which was inexplicable.

Very soon my husband and I were safely on our "inner journeys"—he working with a woman and I with a man. The man that I saw reminded me very much of my grandfather, a big man, seated in his big chair, puffing on his pipe, saying little, but seeming very deep and wise—a kind of Swiss-Gentile grandfather. He would grunt and comment sparingly, but he kept my nose to my own inner work and gave me the atmosphere for the deep and clear questioning of myself that I needed so much at the time. My husband and I had a number of friends, of course, and good ones, whom we saw often, but the main thing was "the work."

Mornings one would get up, write down one's dreams, and "work on them," then go to analysis and then to classes. After lunch and chats with friends in the restaurants, one would have another class, come back home to read and study. The evenings would be free for talk, good students' talk, or study, or cafes, or movies. It was a good life and we loved it.

What of the search into my soul? After the initial searching into the darkness, it became clear that part of my darkness was that I knew just too little—that I had been insufficiently educated. I needed to read and to study, and so I did. I studied at the Institute and I studied at the university as well. I studied psychology, of course. I very much resented the idea that I might be a psychologist or become an analyst, like my husband, because that seemed too much like following his path, and I wanted babies anyway. My soul insisted otherwise. It seemed to say that part of my barrenness was lack of education and that I had to study. I had a "big dream" in which a Voice with great authority told me that I was to become a psychotherapist. The authority of this voice was such that it could not be denied. I tried to reject it and promptly got quite ill with diarrhea and nausea. When I accepted the "voice," the illness cleared up at once. Both my analyst and my husband agreed with the "voice"—another example of male solidarity—and I had to submit.

I must confess that once I embarked on this path, I did not find it disagreeable. The work was hard but interesting, and there were, of course, those lovely long vacations in spring and summer when we could travel all over Europe and see the great historical and cultural wonders—plus, of course, the cafes, the people, the food. It was fine!

I studied, I learned, I analyzed, and I seemed to be following "my path". Still I was "barren" and the great inner darkness would make itself felt as an unknown cloud in my dreams, or a door unopened, and I could not get at it. Using the techniques of "active fantasy," of carrying on a dialogue with the figures of dreams and fantasy, even this great technique of the Mater, failed to bring this gloomy darkness into the full light of consciousness. I uncovered much and understood my childhood, my relation with my parents, especially that with my father. I relived and healed the neurosis of my adolescence and I "developed," but I could not reach the darkness or the barrenness.

In time, I completed my studies at the University, was myself a Doctor, just like my husband. It felt very strange to be one. I felt that I was not at all intelligent, nor able, but I did understand a few things and believed that I might be able to help people with my care and concern, if not my capacity to understand intellectually. My husband had enough of that for both of us!

After 1957, I was fully occupied with the Institute and my post-doctoral studies to become an analyst and psycho-therapist. Our other life became less and less important—and the only big event was the war which Israel quickly won against the Arabs. It was over so quickly that we had no chance to go home and fight. We were delighted with the outcome, of course, and sorry that we had not helped. We were also glad to be out of the wars and concerns of the world, safely covered up in our little nest. It is amazing, now that I think of it, how much we both needed that period of nesting! I am not clear, even yet, why we needed it so much, but it was deeply life-giving at the time.

Still, there was no answer to the deep darkness. Yes, there was a good deal of inner light—I was much more aware of myself, of the world, of the history of the spirit and of the development of consciousness. I was aware of my roots and what had formed me and of my commitments, but still...

It seemed to have to do with the problem of evil; the problem of six million dead Jews. More personally, it had to do with the death of my brothers, who would have been so much more creative and valuable than I. Why was I alive and they dead? Was what my grandfather said true? That I was meant to be like the ancient Sarah, to have children when old? If so, why? There seemed to be no answer to these questions, no matter how hard I, or my analyst, worked.

It sounds as if only superficial things were dealt with in my analysis, or, if deep, that the deepest part of me was untouched – the part where the essential darkness was. If that is the impression which I am giving, I wish to correct it. No, that is not the case. Indeed, let me say that I finally understood the paradox under which I had been living for so long: that I was an atheist and chosen to be one by God. I understood it somewhat as follows: Man has always had a God, and this image of God is really a projection of the Self, his own totality, the ruling principle within his own psyche, of himself and the world, of which he is unconscious. The image of God, in short, is a psychological projection like any other, though its potency and mystery and importance are greater than any other. I understood that man's image of God changes in accordance with his general development. I also understood that his general development is contingent on his environment, on his society, and on the way he makes his living. In short, the Marxist part of me was also satisfied, but at another level. Man is conditioned by his society and his history and it is real, but not only material in the way Marx saw it. He, like an alchemist, was projecting his visions into matter: it is real, but psychic. I also saw that man needed Community, or *communitas*, in the Christian sense, and that modern man, having lost it, needed it desperately.

I understood the paradox that "God had chosen me to be an atheist and a Communist" to be translated into a statement that the Self, the highest totality of me, had selected the function my ego to be a challenger of all current and past images of this totality (God), and that I was meant, by this same unknown and unknowable totality, to reject all of those current images of God. In short, when people said, "God is dead," they were saying the psychological truth that the old image of God was no longer viable or believable. My task was to deny all images, even the image which transcended images. *That I am the atheist for God means nothing less than that I serve that image of God which is beyond all images, beyond all past, present and future understandings, in short that I am indeed Jewish, and have no images of God at all!*

That, to my delight, makes me, indeed, a Jewish atheist for God!

My Communism became clear to me, too, in the sense which I have already given it. We are all brothers and sisters. We live under the same archetypal and general psychological reality. We are meant to live together in that foreseeable future when men and women will be brothers and sisters on earth. Again the paradox of a Jew who can be a Communist is resolved: The Jewish image of Heaven realized on Earth at the coming of the Messiah! Such a Communist, in hope, am I!

So now, when I quote what I said in the beginning: "There is only one life, we have to improve conditions on this dreary planet, and mankind has to evolve and produce paradise on earth, not individual men and not God" – these words, indeed, sound atheist and Communist, and indeed they are, but now you will understand that they come from a religious and psychological atheist and communist, which is quite an individual matter, indeed!

These solutions are far from superficial, in my opinion, but they still did not reach that ultimate blackness of which I have spoken. I could not solve the problem of evil entirely! All the same, I had come to some inner acceptance, understanding, and reconciliation.

With this relative peace and understanding, I thought that perhaps my understanding of evil was much too dark, and that now, in truth, I might become fertile, as my grandfather had said that I would. We were, in point of fact, nearing the end of our stay in Switzerland, and had less than a year to complete our studies. In the midst of this relative peace and under-standing, my husband painfully told me that he had been deeply attracted to another and had been unfaithful to me.

I was seared to the depths of my being. Evil was no longer an academic issue, intellectual; nor was it a personal issue of my own darkness, as well—I had been through too much of that in my analysis. No, evil was worse. Evil was the pain of guilt and fear, and of being torn apart into little pieces! I suddenly realized the guilt of my having insufficiently cared for my husband. I realized the guilt of deep and dark possessiveness, and of not wanting him to live, nor myself. I felt the fear of his leaving me; I felt the fear of being alone; I felt the fear of being thought of as a fool; I felt the humiliation of all of it. And throughout, I felt love. I wanted him to do what he had to do; I felt strangely open to him as I had never felt before; I felt torn apart and open at the same time. I felt as if I had been raped by life. That was the evil: I was confronted with the ultimate darkness of betrayal and of love and openness at the same time. Worst of all, I knew that my husband was, in his way, in the same place. I did not understand it altogether, nor did I want to know, really, but I knew that he loved me and did what he must.

In the midst of the suffering and agony, I walked again in the forest. The forests here were much like those of my childhood, and I had often gone to them on the outskirts of the city, for solace, meditation, or joy. Now I went in agony and desperation. Whatever I did was wrong: that was the greatest evil of all. In the midst of my agony, I had the fantasy of my grandfather coming to me, He was full of infinite compassion and care. Tears welled in his eyes as he patted my head and comforted me. After a time, I stopped crying, and he said, "Julia, as I told you, you will be as Sarah. I can only tell you, that until today, you have been as Sarai, loyal and true and devoted, and a handmaiden. Now you have felt God's darkness and you have been impregnated in the spirit. Just as Sarai became Sarah, you, in truth, will, inside of yourself, change from Julia to Juliah. You have felt the spirit of the Lord. Now you will, yourself, be the mother of new creations. You will suffer much, but you will create."

My grandfather vanished, in the fantasy. I really felt that he was a ghost, coming from the dead. After that, I had a measure of peace.

That night, I was impregnated by my husband and I knew that I had been touched by both man and God. Atheist, yes; Communist, yes; but now I had *known* God, as Sarah had known Abraham, and I was a girl no more.

The depth of this experience made me more silent than ever. The few remaining months of our stay in Switzerland were largely those of getting ready to leave—saying goodbye to friends and so on. Only one event had the significance of this depth. That was my final visit with the Great Psychologist. I had completed my studies, as had my husband, and we each, in our time, had arranged to have a final interview with him. My husband's came first and, when he returned, he seemed serene. He apparently had gotten what he wanted or needed and was at peace with himself. When I went, it was strange. I was very quiet, could hardly bring myself to face him, feeling a great numinosity in being with him, yet shy and embarrassed. We chatted a bit for a time, in which I told him that I had found his books difficult to read. He answered, "They were difficult to write." I told him of one which had moved me the most and he nodded and sighed, and said that that was the most difficult, painful, yet important experience—the deepest confrontation with evil. At that point, I burst into tears. I could not help myself and wept uncontrollably. The Great Psychologist, Swiss and Gentile as he was, proved to be much like my grandfather. He waited quietly, did not even ask me why I was crying, but then began to speak in a quiet voice about himself, his own life and sufferings: his voyages, experiences, even to his betrayals and being betrayed. I looked up in wonder. Now I knew that he was a great man, and not just a Great Psychologist, for he spoke to my condition, from a depth within his own, from an instinct which was just right. He risked all. He risked being a fool, a madman, and presumptuous, but he nad infinite regard, I felt, for my suffering, and for his own, and did not intrude. In short, where I had been raped by God, he lovingly repaired this rape. He did so out of his own experience of being raped by the same God. I came away healed.

VI

In 1960 my husband and I left Switzerland. I had finished the fifth seven -year cycle of my life, and was now deeply aware of how this cyclic character had affected me. For reasons of my husband's career and his own inner calling (for he had his own deeply religious experiences during this period), we had to go back to America to live, rather than return to Israel. I had no such calling, but like Ruth, felt it deep in myself, deep in my own being, to go wither my husband would go.

We returned to America and started our life there. True to my experience, I had been impregnated that night and, in regular time, I gave birth to a lovely daughter. I was much fulfilled, though I felt a twinge at not having provided both my husband and my grandfather with a son. I laughed, though, and realized that, luckily, I was not Sarah, but Julia, after all, and I was not about to have an Isaac like her. I knew that I had gone through an archetypal experience like her, but, thank goodness, did not have to live her faith. Obvious evidence: I was thirty-four when I had my first child, and not in my nineties!

In the years that immediately followed, my husband and I adjusted rather well to the new life. He had been an American, so it was both easier for him, and more painful to come back to the land where he had never felt at home with his soul and spirit. I knew that my spirit and soul did not belong there, but also knew that the "flesh" was there, and I was having children in the flesh. I discovered that for a woman, children of the flesh are one's real homecoming and that is the first and initial task. All the rest could come later.

It was enough for me for several years. I had two daughters and then two sons, twins! With the sons, I had a dream that I was with "the Mothers." I was with my mother, who was still living in actuality, with a grandmother, and with a great and unknown creature, who was, I suppose, the Great mother. We were all laughing with joy. These two sons seemed recompense for my two brothers. It was a secret among us that the souls of my two sons were, in actuality, the souls of my brothers. So I was mother to my brothers reborn! I was sister to my mother, and wife of my father! Incestual things in the spirit; shocking, I suppose, but deeply satisfying within.

I had not solved the collective problem of Six million dead Jews, but I felt, in my soul, that two of them were reborn through me!

For several years, I was fully involved in caring for my children and making a comfortable home for my husband. The spirit of our home was good and warm and it felt like the good days of my childhood in the Forest, though now we had several rooms and not even one goat! We had dogs and cats, instead, with an occasional bird, turtle, or lizard, cared for by our children.

After four years, our financial situation had much improved, as such things do in America—that is one of the great things about it—and we were even having luxuries. The children's needs much occupied me, but I began to have spiritual longings which were unsatisfied. At that time, my husband and I took a trip to Europe and Israel for a holiday and to visit our friends. I saw my old analyst and had a dream—how convenient for me, don't you think?—that showed clearly that I should begin to practice the work for which I had been prepared: psychotherapy. I laughed about this "convenience," and upon our return, I did begin to see patients. At first I worked only a few hours per week, but with time and as my children spent more time in school, on a larger scale.

This work proved absorbing for me. All that I learned was put to the test and there was a new place of connection between my husband and myself. We did not wish to discuss the patients, themselves, but to discuss our feelings and reactions, dreams and situations. Our relationship was much better, yet I was aware that my maternal feelings were mobilized much more readily by my children and my patients than by him. The problem of the "fathers" and of the "mothers" had been greatly healed for me, in analysis, in being a mother myself, in bringing me closer to my own mother, but there were still areas in which I was deficient.

During some of this later period, I was able to stand by my husband better, as he went through betrayals of various kinds, even at the hands of those whom he loved and thought he was loved by. I now knew that he was experiencing what I had experienced some years before. I could not put this into words for him, but I knew it, and I felt that he knew that I knew it.

My feeling, deep as it was, was now beginning to be felt all around me. I was less afraid to express it and it was having its effect. My husband's experiences, however, were also having an effect upon me. How could it be that these people, people that he had known and loved and, presumably, had also loved him—how could they betray him so and not even be aware of it? I fully understood the inner grief and agony of betrayal. I understood, too, that one might not know what to do about it, but I could not comprehend their lack of consciousness, their righteousness.

My thoughts went deep. Were these people, like the Communists, about to destroy my faith in psychology? My faith in communism had been challenged and destroyed by my experience of Communists, who had proved to be greedy, power-driven and, in some ways, more frightening than non-Communists. Were psychologists—those who through insight and self-knowledge were going to be the inheritors of the future kingdom on earth—were these people going to disappoint me? Were they not living up to my expectations, just as the Communists had done? Yes, of course. Now I had to think more deeply, about both my communism and my psychology.

I had resolved the paradox of my atheism in a deeply satisfying way. Being an atheist for God, as I have said, was enduringly satisfying. Shall I say it again? Yes, I shall: "I am an atheist of God, which means nothing less than that I serve that image of God which is beyond all images, beyond all past, present or future understandings, in short that I am indeed Jewish, and have no images of god at all!"

This, as I say, was deeply satisfying for my atheism, but I had no such deeply satisfying understanding of my communism, except in the future "brotherhood of man" when the Messiah comes. Somehow, this statement seemed inadequate to me. It was all right some six years earlier, but now it seemed thin, in comparison to the enduring symbol and understanding of my atheism.

What is more, the communism and the psychology were drawn together, or identical, in a way which surpassed my understanding. More and more, this intellectual dilemma occupied me. Was I forever doomed to have my ideals shattered by the realities of life? It was true that my experience of the "rape" by God was tremendous, but one of those per lifetime seemed enough. Yes, my grandfather had assured me that I would suffer, but I did not feel that such a particular kind of suffering had to be relived.

So what did it mean that psychologists failed to be psychologists and Communists failed to be communists, and yet these two viewpoints had within them the highest ideals of my life: individual development and totality for the psychologist, and collective joy and redemption for the Communist. Perhaps my idealism was at fault—I expected too much, of others, of myself, and even of the realization of ideas. Yet, where had my own "creativity" come, when had I become impregnated? When I was torn apart by the divine paradox, by the good and evil in God? I could take the good and evil in God, but I could not take it in man? Yes, that was it! What presumption! I could accept that God was both good and evil, but man, somehow, had to be better; had, even, to be better than God!

So, I thought, is that the flaw in my reasoning? Is that why I cannot come to a deeper place in my communism and psychology? Because of the inflation and expectation? Yes, they are neither one very individual, are they? In which case my psychological views fail in the very thing that they admire, they are not individual! And my communism fails in the opposite direction; it is not very communal!

What shall I do about it? Develop my own psychological theory and thus satisfy the ultimate demands of my psychological ideals? Go out and save the world, or, at least, a part of it, and thus satisfy my Communist ideals? Both of these sounded wrong to me—the first because I had no new theory, really, and the second because it is very much against my temperament. What to do, therefore?

I found myself in this state of mind when the Arab states were once again threatening my beloved Israel. Israel was all alone, but, in lightning-like fashion, like the Maccabees of old, they whirled through the opposition and captured all, with a minimum of loss of life. All my old Kibbutzniks were in it and I loved them. How my husband and I wanted to join them and fight! But we could not. Now the Communists everywhere were against Israel and I knew that all the outer communism was the enemy of my deepest identification—spiritual, soul or flesh. Yet I could not abandon my ideal: all men are as brothers—to each what he needs, from each what he has to offer.

In this state of mind, I went to sleep. I dreamed—or, at least, I think I dreamed. For I found myself in this forest, or one very like it. Because to tell you the truth I do not know if I am dreaming. I do not know if all of you are parts of my dream or if, in fact, I am part of yours. No, I am almost caught in solipsism which does not hold water. I know only that I am here, and that I have had such and such experiences. I will leave it to someone else to determine whether it is inner or outer. Let me, then, simply go on with my story.

I went to sleep then, and dreamt that I was in a forest. In the dream, I felt relieved to be in a nice green forest again, which was like those of Poland an Switzerland—ordered and tended and not so wild as those in America—and I could sit down and rest. In my dream, I rested long by the water and drank deeply thereof. At that point in my dream, I dreamt that I fell asleep and had a dream. It was a dream within a dream, hence my confusion. In my dream, I saw my grandfather smiling at me and embracing me. After him, came the Great Psychologist, who did the same. Then came the turn of my father and I wept to see him again. There was a short pause as I thought of how I had missed him. Then I embraced the three men and they embraced me. We made a circle and bowed our heads together. The circle then broke and my husband appeared. He smiled and I ran to him and embraced him and he held my hand. Suddenly my two dead brothers appeared, as if in the flesh, and I gasped as I saw them. As I went forward to touch their hands, they changed into my two sons, back and forth, proving that the dead two were the living two. I was overcome with all of this, when all the men, led by my grandfather, united in a circle. Grandfather, father, psychologist, husband, brothers, sons—all six of them turned into two triangles which joined together as a Star of David—a living Star of David—and I knew what it meant when one said, God has become Man. They danced a *hora* in a circle and my joy was great. Their circle changed from the dance to the Star—back and forth. As it did so, I became aware of my grandmother, smiling at me, too. "Bubeh," I cried out and ran to her. Just behind her was my mother, holding in each hand the little hand of each of my daughters. I joined the women and we all held hands and danced a *hora* of our own, laughing and calling out to the men in the other circle. We were five, they were six, and they all were ten—my own *minyan*—plus me. We made a very large circle—all eleven of us—and danced until we were hot and tired and exhausted. When I thought my heart would burst with happiness, a strange thing happened. Suddenly, there was a silence. The men withdrew and formed a line; we women withdrew and formed a half-circle. To my astonishment, our feminine half-circle, which was moon-like, became a sickle; and the line of men became a kind of hammer. The men invaded us, and together we made a hammer and sickle: the Communist symbol. At that moment, my father spoke and said, "This is our Commune, that of family and those who love each other. We welcome into it all who belong there. It is not family alone, or Jewish alone, for is not the Great Psychologist with us, too? Ours is the beginning of the family of man and the brotherhood of man, both potential and actual. We will live the actual and hope for the potential."

The Great Psychologist then spoke and said, "What you see as the height of you ideal, and your attitude and your way, the Communist hammer and sickle, is to me, dear friends, a Psi—that Greek sign of my ideal devotion, psychology, the study and devotion of the soul. That is in the service of the Self and of men. So, I embrace you."

I awakened from the dream within the dream and found myself here in your forest. It is not Paradise to me, or is it? And it is not a dream to me, or is it?

I do see your tree, Sir Knight, and it is amazing! I see there...do you see it? I see the hammer and sickle—that symbol of work and the brotherhood of men, and I see that it is also a psi. I see that it is psychology that unites them and what more can I say? For the great Psychologist has said it, and my father has said it, and Knight, good Knight, you do, indeed, seem like my brother and I embrace you. And you good Arab, and good Ronin, you are my brothers, and I am you sister, for you, too, as my father said, belong in my circle, do you not? Yes, you do! My symbol fits yours, does it not? Yes, it does!

THE MEDIUM, SOPHIE-SARAH

I

My name is Sophie-Sarah. As a child and youth I was also called
"gypsy," "fortune-teller," "Madame Sophie" and "Sophie, the Medium." As
you might guess from this, I have dabbled in the occult. But before I speak
of that, I feel that I must tell you something of my background. The story of
my personal life is less central to why I am here, I think, but I must tell you
about "Who I Am" as I discovered it through the great crisis of my life,
which involved the occult.

I am well past fifty years old, but still look attractive, if I do say so
myself. I was born in Romania, but conceived in Spain, before the First
World War. My father was a talented but rather impractical inventor of
Russian-Jewish extraction and my mother was a very strong Austro-
Hungarian lady who combined the vitality and cleverness of her Jewish
father (a business man), and the beauty and intensity of her Greek mother. I
have, in point of fact, inherited not only my name from my grandmothers
(Sophia was my Greek grandmother's name and Sarah was my father's
mother's name) but also many of their traits. I was dark and intense and
pretty, like my mother's mother, and impractical and dreamy like my
father's mother. The point, though, is that in temperament and in appearance, I was more like a Spanish gypsy than anything else. Much of my life
has been an internal struggle between gypsy and Jew.

I do not think that this conflict was engendered simply because I was
conceived in Spain on a honeymoon trip and subject to the astrological
influences surrounding the moment of conception. Rather, I firmly believe
that I have lived several previous lives in Spain and that it was, in fact, the
unsolved problems of these previous lives that were evoked by the chance
event that my Jewish parents happened to spend their honeymoon there.

So, you see, I believe in reincarnation. No, that is not quite right: I
know that there is reincarnation, but I know it for myself and neither can
nor wish to prove it to anyone else. I shall have more to say about these
previous lives in Spain and what they meant to me, but first I must tell you
about the course of my present life.

I was a dreamy child. I liked to tell myself stories and to perform all
sorts of magical tricks. I had a temper and was inclined to stormy outbursts.
My parents were very good about both sides of me, allowing me to indulge

my imaginative activity as a creative pastime and accepting my emotional intensity without spoiling me or encouraging pseudo-dramatics. I thus had a healthy upbringing and was enormously loved by and loving toward both of my parents. From what I have seen of my generation in Europe and America, I realize that my experience of family love and understanding was not at all typical. The separation between generations seems to grow wider and wider, but this was not true for me, nor for my children, or grandchildren.

The intensity and dreaminess, however, fostered a mystical and wild streak in me and inclined me more toward self-examination than might have been my nature otherwise. Other than that, I was quite normal. I was deeply loved by my parents, as I have said, had plenty of good food and comfort, friends, a good education, and was not deprived of my fantasy.

Throughout my childhood and adolescence, my parents and I wandered all over Europe, especially around the Mediterranean, in search of support for one or another of my father's inventions. Some of these inventions were successful, some not, but my mother made up for his impracticality with her ability to sew, to paint, and to charm people. We always had plenty of money, though few lasting relationships.

But I, what was I? From the age of nine or ten onwards, I was everybody's gypsy, astrologer, palmist, medium. At first it was a game I played; people indulged the cute play of the pretty child. As time went on, there was a growing belief in my "powers"; adults, even my parents, grew to respect me and to put value on my "gifts." This was particularly surprising because, at least until the advent of Hitler, World War II and the Holocaust, most people were highly rationalistic and very suspicious, if not downright hostile, toward anything "occult." Because of the irrational destructiveness of Hitler and the horrors of the Holocaust, people do not ridicule the irrational as they did, particularly the irrationally destructive. Imagine, then what such a rationalistic environment, giving adulation to a "mystical" and "gifted" child might do to her.

Can you imagine? It inflated me. Well, I was, as I say, a healthy child, so by the time I was in my middle teens and beginning to be more involved with boys and love than with astral journeys, I tried to get away from that kind of attention from others to me. It wasn't easy. I could accomplish this only by convincing the others and myself that it was all a fake, that I was no medium and had no powers of predicting the future, reading character, or the like.

When Hitler came to power in 1933, my parents evaluated what was happening and wisely decided to emigrate to the United States. I used that change of milieu to change my personality. From the age of 19 onwards, I turned away from the occult and tried to live a conventional life. It was easy for me. At first, in America, my parents encouraged me to continue to dabble in the occult. I tried to convince them that it was all fake and I nearly succeeded, but, I am afraid, I convinced myself more than I did them. Nonetheless, life went on happily for me, by and large.

I later married a man who was a psychologist and, for a time, I flirted again with my mediumship by taking an interest in his projective methods of personality diagnosis. I would occasionally look at the results of his Rorschach tests and say more about his subjects and patients than he was able to tell from his more rational, scientific methods. Since he is very intuitive himself, this was no ordinary accomplishment. I grew afraid of this talent (thinking it pseudo) and backed away from it. I satisfied myself with the raising of our four lovely children. I had been an only child and very much wanted to have several children, not because I had been lonely as a child, but because I wanted the experience of family life and roots, rather than "specialness" and "wandering." We had friends and a good life together, including the usual problems and pains of all human beings. We were lucky enough, however, to be spared the greater pains, such as loss of a child or other loved ones; or poverty, or disgrace. No, we had none of these.

So, for the most part, my life has been usual, except for the particular experiences that I have been having over the last several years. These have had to do with the occult and it is because of these occurrences, I think, that I find myself here among you.

About three years ago, I began having strange dreams and sleepless nights. I had always been a good dreamer and prided myself on my ability to interpret or cope with my dreams in such a way that I could use them in my development. I did this without the help of an analyst or books. Occasionally, I asked my husband what he thought of a dream and would profit from his reactions, but otherwise, I worked pretty much alone. In the past, some of my dreams had been deep or "big," but these new dreams were different. They were of another order than the ones I had theretofore. These dreams seemed more like objective events, coming to me from outside myself. I had known about the "objective psyche," both from reading and from my husband, who was an analyst trained in the method of C.G. Jung. I had tried Jung's ways of understanding dreams, as I have said, and had found them very satisfactory. But these dreams were different. Surely, they were like the "objective psyche" but they seemed more concrete, more specific, more detailed than the symbolic reality that Jung had written about and that I had experienced earlier. I shall have more to say about these dreams later on, because they played a large role in my subsequent experiences.

In addition, I began to have unexplained intensity of feelings: deep depression and wild elation. I had always been emotionally intense and had lived deeply, both alone and with others, but these swings were different. Was I undergoing another "change of life?" I had experienced the physiological "change" without incident some years earlier. Was I experiencing first stages of madness? Neither was true. I knew in my heart that neither was true, but I needed reassurance, so I went to respected scientific sources for help. A medical friend convinced himself and me that I was not organically ill by giving me a complete physical examination. A psychologist friend was kind enough to give me a battery of tests, which convinced us both that I was not losing my mind.

I was thrown back upon myself. I could easily have confided in my husband what was going on inside of me. Indeed, I had kept him fully informed until this point, but he seemed to worry too much about me and I saw that this might well take him away from all the important duties in his life, as well as take away the pleasures and joys of our relationship otherwise. In deepest truth, however, I really wanted to be utterly alone with these new experiences. Some unformulated voice was stirring in me. It was saying that it wanted me to take on its message quite alone, at least for a time, and that I should share it with no one else, not even my husband. So, with some trepidation, I accepted this internal hint and waited in silence.

After a time, several strands of word-fantasy began to make themselves clear. They would repeat, as questions, or as commands. Sometimes it would be "Read Kabbalah!" or "The Ten Commandments must be reinterpreted." At other times there would be a wail of moaning, as if the dead were coming back to cry to me. But through all of it came a persistent question: *"Six million dead Jews. Why six million dead Jews?"* Sometimes the question came quietly as if in despairing resignation. Sometimes it came as a demand that I answer this question at once, with the implication that if I did not answer adequately, I would be killed. Again the question came as if God, Himself, Blessed be He, were being asked the question and I was present to hear the answer. Still again, the question came as if all Jews were silently posing this question to themselves, to the world, and to God.

In all of these ways the question came. It came with ever-increasing persistence and intensity. I had great difficulty understanding why this question was presented to me, as if either I must answer it or I must ask it of God. I had not suffered the Holocaust of Hitler and the concentration camps personally. Some remote relatives, it is true, had died in the ovens, and I was saddened by that, of course, but I had not personally suffered a family loss.

Like every Jew, I was overjoyed with the advent of Israel. Like most Jews, however, I also felt my identity as a human being as well as a Jew, did not plan to go to Israel to live and—when I did think of these things— thought more about the unity of mankind, the plight of black people, of the poor and hungry and oppressed of Asia, than I did about the fate of the Jews.

So, I wondered, why was I chosen for this question? Then I laughed. Are not the Jews "chosen?" Without regard to their virtue or the justice of it? Do not Jews customarily answer a question with a question? Of course.

And that, perhaps, was why God chose me, just because I was Jewish, and could question and, maybe, could laugh.

But my laughter died in my cheeks. A chill overcame me as I thought of my childhood "mediumship" and the games I had played with it. Suddenly I felt a deep shame for the tricks and games that I had played with my occult talent. I cried all day, and the next, and felt an increasing agony. Even in the midst of my agony. I knew that I was being unfair to myself, or, rather that something in me was being unfair to me. Why was I so seriously responsible for playing like a gypsy or medium in my childhood? Do not other children play this way, too? Why should I be so hard on myself?

The answer came coldly and deeply, without compassion: I had a gift which I had rejected. In order to be like all other children, in order to be assimilated into community life and to be an ordinary girl, I had abandoned the gift of God. For God had given me this gift of mediumship and relation with the occult. I had been chosen just for this. It was important. How many Jews had God chosen for their mediumship? Not many. Not many since the Witch of Endor. God chose the Jews as prophets, and as rabbis, doctors and scientists. That He did often enough. He also chose them as victims and as His Son. But He did not frequently choose them to be gypsy-witches and occult transmitters. He didn't do that because He did not much approve of Jews doing that, and I was not certain if He cared for it in anybody else, either. At least the Jewish God did not like it. But I, in any case, had been so chosen and had misused and then rejected my calling. I had sold my birthright for the security of middle-class life.

God, apparently, could accept "ordinariness" less than anything else. At least from Jews. Jews had to be "special." I had rejected my specialness and I had better reconsider. These thoughts, I was convinced, came from something beyond my own ego. If they did not come from God Himself, they came from an internal authority that I had to respect.

I realized that I must accept my mediumship, and use it in a way which would be acceptable to God, or to that authority inside me which was connected with that same talent. When I submitted to the truth of this realization, I immediately received another message from within, which let me see that I had spent several previous lifetimes in Spain, been a gypsy, a fortune-teller and a medium several times before. Incarnations back, I had even been a male, a deeply mystical Jew who had known Moses de Leon, the writer of the Zohar, and had made great strides in coming to know the God of the Kabbalah. Later on, I had been a gypsy who had used her occult powers badly, for her own selfish ends, and this was the real reason that I was so shy of using my talent in this lifetime. I remembered only too well how I had betrayed my calling when I pretended to contact the dead, for money and for prestige. My body had suffered greatly because of this, and I had painful leg amputations, loss of beauty, and a death in pain and ugliness. On another occasion, I had been called a witch and burned at the stake, but my witchery had been true: I had abused a real talent for the sake of power and evil.

All of this revealed a neglected part of myself as a woman, involved with the occult. It opened up an area which had long been neglected by God, Himself, as we witness from the Bible. He had encouraged it, all the same, even among the Jews, in Kabbalah. In short, it became clear that God's left hand and right hand were doing different things.

These new things preoccupied me. I once again began reading in the occult and I tentatively opened myself to my mediumship.

Promptly as I opened myself, I had two dreams. The first one was as follows:

Many women come to me from the occult world, the "after-world." I am told that I am going to expand more and more in that direction, and that my powers will increase greatly. What had once been "witchy," negative, and fraudulent would take on a positive quality. A dark woman with very dark eyes comes to me and looks deeply into my own. Is she my "self?" End of dream.

Some days later I dreamt the following:

I am deep, deep, beneath the worlds of Gehenna, of Hell. I am looking at backsides. At this deep, deep place, I am given the *mitzvah* by God to speak about and explain the *Shoah*, the Holocaust. It is denied everywhere. They say: "How is this possible; how can one speak who has not concretely suffered it?" But it is true. I will speak because I am so ordained by God. And it is so, via the dead, through six million who want to speak, through the medium. End of dream.

The second dream was just in those words, and I could not make it any different. Thus it was that my crisis of being occurred, and thus it was that I was led into...

II

"...and thus it was that I was led into..." I could not finish these words. For some days I was suspended, not knowing what it was I was being "led into." Nor can I tell you now that I know for certain where I was led. I was not told that it was Hell or Purgatory, or any such place, though I believe that it was a kind of Gehenna. Nay, I know that it was a Gehenna, but I also believe that there are several Gehinnom, many states and circles of being. "Planes of existence" is the phrase I have heard somewhere, and that, too, is what I mean, not in a pale theosophical sense, but as a living reality.

So, then, I was led into a Gehenna in which I beheld a vision. The vision was of a vast number of people suffering in agony. They were in all states of torment, twisting in agonizing pain. They were starved and burned and heated in furnaces. They were being humiliated. Little boys were hanging from ropes by their necks; little girls were forced to watch their mothers being raped. It was all of the flesh, yet all the figures were as wraiths. I knew that all of these were living images of the *Shoah*, the Holocaust. The people were undergoing the agonies of the unspeakable Hells which were inflicted upon them. I knew that these were images of the past, the living images of torment and despair as they had existed historically and would exist for eternity. This sin against mankind would exist forever and could not be expunged. Yet I knew—and do not ask how I knew this, it was given to me to know in as real a way as the fact that I am here to tell you what I experienced—I knew that the living beings who had experienced all these horrors were no longer here. They were mercifully on other planes of existence. They had either already been reborn in new lives on earth, or in other states of being. In short, they had been reincarnated in various states and were free from the horrors that they had endured.

Yet the horror continued. What did it mean? I became aware that just above the grey sea of suffering humanity was a figure of a little man, standing at a lectern. He was gesticulating and preaching and raving in a highly emotional state, trying to affect this mass of people. His drama was extraordinary: He would raise his arms up high; he would clasp his hands together in front of his chest with an anguished show of feeling and intensity; he would let his arms drop between his knees, as if summoning up all the truths from the depths, with conviction, to make his point. The man wept, he snorted, he cried; he spoke deeply and seriously; he spoke softly and reasonably. He went on and on.

I could not make out his face. It was vague. I strained my eyes and then moved in closer. Can you not guess who it was I saw? Can you not imagine who it was who spoke in such a highly dramatic way? Who else would be require to suffer the pain of Hell in this way? To preach one's message to the despairing, suffering souls to whom one has caused unspeakable anguish, pain, and humiliation? It was, of course, Adolf Hitler.

I thought: How sensible a punishment. No, not a punishment, since no punishment could possibly repay that man for the pain and destruction he had caused. No, it was a kind of ironic truth. That man had a mission, a belief; he was, he thought, a messiah for the people of the earth. Let him, now, convince his victims of his vision. Let him, now, be allowed the full use of his powers; let him see the pain and anguish and misery he has caused. It occurred to me that Hitler perhaps never grasped the immensity of all the pain and anguish and misery he had caused, because it would have killed him on the spot. Who among us can really see all the pain we have caused and allow it to continue? None, for we must all rationalize it and say that it is for a higher cause or in proper retribution and other such explanations. But here is Hitler, required to explain, testify and convince his victims, for eternity. They cannot be convinced, of course, can they?

Or can they? What is eternity after all? Can any of us really conceive of what eternity is? Is not the anguish of unbearable pain an eternity when it is more than an instant? Or, oppositely, the impossibility of containing the ecstasies of love for more than a little while, without bursting? What good is the eternity of punishment? Is this what the Lord, blessed and praised be He, wants? Does He get pleasure from endless retribution? Does an "eye for an eye, tooth for a tooth" mean just that? Must we forever remain with that level of justice, a primitive kind of vengeance? Even when we rationally add that the Lord meant no *more* than an eye for an eye, no *more* than a tooth for a tooth? Yes, and a life for a life? No *more* than that?

So, while I contemplated the vision of Hitler explaining himself and preaching to his victims, I began to have thoughts of the deity, Himself. What kind of a God was this, to permit the horror of six million dead Jews? So, my thoughts turned from Hitler to God.

I thought that I saw Hitler with one eye. He was God Himself. Hitler was alive, as God was alive. God must be a madman, continually causing destruction and catastrophe with His unconsciousness of Himself, just like Hitler. For why else would He permit such destruction to occur?

So, I was asking, for the first time, "Why six million dead Jews?" The answer was beginning to filter down to me. This image of Hitler was like the pictures one had seen in the films, the voice one had heard on the radio. But it was also like the lectures I had heard from certain German Jews. I remember an "assimilationist" speaking at a lecture, seeming very much like Hitler in his manner. I recalled encountering other Jews who were like Hitler. They were weak, pompous little men, jealous of their power, for they had very little of it personally but used and identified with the power of their office or institution. Or they were devious and unable to face a person directly. They were rigid and moralizing and unmoving. I remembered them and I felt revulsion.

"And God made man in his own image." All of these, then, are images of God. Then Hitler, too, is an image of God. Is it not God who is being made to face the horror of His works? Good, then let God face His own destructiveness and unconsciousness! Good, then let us, mankind, cry out to the living God to face his horribleness!

God is not dead! That is an impertinence! God is too horrible to die! He ought to live forever just to see how horrible He is! It is just that our old images of God have to die. Even the image that Job had must die, and he had the most profound one after Moses, did he not?

I remembered then from Kabbalah that only Moses had a true intercourse with God. It was Moses who saw God "face to face" and was transfigured thereby. The story was that once he had this "intercourse," he would no longer have "intercourse" with his wife. Shades of Freud, who also gave up sexual union with his wife, once he had his own vision. Job, my thoughts went on, had seen the "backside" of God. He alone was vouchsafed that vision. The consequence, as Jung had taught us, was God having to become Man. The first Messiah had come and Christianity resulted thereby.

What, now, would God do about all mankind seeing His "backside?" Not only did Job see the backside of God, in His plot with the devil, in his unconsciousness and in his vast display of unrelated power, but all mankind has now seen this! They, and we, know what a Hitler you are, Lord! We know that You are rotten and self-involved, concerned only about Your own power and visions and cannot even cope with the worm of man. We see this, now, and what are You going to do about it? Send another Holocaust? How many would you like?

Such were my thoughts as I contemplated the figure of Hitler speaking to the multitudes of suffering Jews. And I knew the answer, or thought I did. God must be so ashamed of His misused power and unconsciousness that He must become man in all of us. Not only His one son of Christ as the Messiah which we Jews had not accepted, but at least in the Six Million Sons and Daughters of the destroyed Jews. What else could He possibly do than enter into the souls of the Six Million more deeply?

I remembered that in Kabbalah it was stated that the original Jews of Mt. Sinai numbered 600,000. Each face and being therein constituted an individual experience of God, and that there were, therefore, 600,000 different interpretations and views of the Torah! How deep and true! But what of the Six million? That is the 600,000, an entire Jewish totality, raised ten times. A totality raised by a *minyan*, another totality. What could it mean? What gematria, what Kabbalistic meaning did this play of numbers intend? That God had given His message to the 600,000. The six hundred thousand had given way to the One, who was the Son of God. But now the One, who was the Son, would give way to the Six Million. There would be, at least, Six Million Sons of God. God must, for His own sake, incarnate in all of them, and in all of us who could bear it. Only this, only this could possibly redeem the horribleness of God! Furthermore, God had to have this, in order to fulfill His own need for consciousness and for humanness.

All this came to me as I viewed the horrible-laughable picture of Hitler preaching to the Jews!... The words, the Six, the Six, kept coming to me. Six is the number of creation. God created man on the Sixth day, and He created man in His own image! The six, the six hundred thousand and the six million. So six is the number of God creating man and, in creating, encountering man, and, in encountering, choosing man and, in choosing, finally, of becoming man. For God has to become human. He has to become one and whole with His creation, which is less sinful than He, blessed be His name!

As I viewed this view and thought these thoughts, I saw the figure of Hitler cease his posturing and gesticulating and his impotent screaming. I saw him desist from this horror and begin to weep. I saw him fall flat on his face before the multitude of Jews. I saw him beg for forgiveness. And I saw the multitude of Jews in their answer. Many, many, fell flat on their faces as well, before the face of the Living God and His Horribleness. They fell and they wept, for they, like I, understood that his horribleness was part of the horribleness and wonder of God becoming incarnated in men. And that this incarnation was greater, by far, than the incarnation of His Son, which had been the last great event in the history of the Jews. For now the incarnation would be total, for every person who would bear it; and which of us could claim that his wielding of power was always good and loving and true? These Jews fell and felt the fall of Adam and his sin, for we were all there, as Kabbalah tells us; we were all there in the first man and woman, and we all participated in that first sin. It was the sin of pride. But now we are justified, for it was God's sin, too. And those among the Jews who saw this were transfigured, for they, too, like Moses, were seeing the image of God, face to face.

But there were those Jews who did not forgive Hitler. There were those Jews so hurt, so mortified, so betrayed, that they could not. In these the rending was so great that they needed aeons of love to soften the pain and dry the blood of their wounds. For them there would be grief and lamentation, despair and excess of love for eternity. That is, for as long as would be needed until their wounds would be healed from all pain.

There were others among the Jews who would not forgive, not out of pain, but out of the same arrogance and conceit, posturing and impotence, which was as Hitler's. They were doomed to suffer as Hitler had suffered; not out of punishment, for that old view should die. No, they were doomed to live their impotence and harshness and stupidity until they could be softened and transformed. For they, too, like the Hitlers and the fools, were sparks of the Divine Image. They, too, had to be transformed through pain and enlightenment, until God, in all of His grandeur and horror can be totally redeemed. And how can God be redeemed until His creatures, those created in His image, are totally transformed? This is the work of the universe. This is the task of the era which comes. This is the meaning of the Water, the Aquarian age, when God will become more totally human. That is the Messiah of us all. That is the work of us all, that God be united with His Shekinah, and we, mankind, are His Shekhinah.

Such was my image, and such was one answer to the question, *"Why six million dead Jews?"*

III

Can there be another answer? Is that not enough? What more can one ask of the Living God? Such were my thoughts for many days after I had this mediumistic experience and revelation. The image of Hitler preaching to the Jews so astounded me and so horribly-laughably gripped me that I lived and re-lived the experience, including his weeping and redemption, many times. It was as if the message—of God becoming Man—was enough for the redemption of the Six Million...

Or was it? Certainly not. It seemed enough for me, but I, of course, had not been among the Six Million, any more than I had been present among the Six Hundred Thousand at the foot of Mt. Sinai. Yet I had been there in spirit, my mediumistic experience had said, as had said the Rabbis, the great Sages among the Kabbalists. I was surely chosen for this strange vision, was I not? Yes.

So, I waited. I waited until the Good Lord, blessed be His Holy Name, would descend unto me and tell me again the answer to the question, "Why Six Million Dead Jews?"

Then I had another vision. It was as if I rose up—no, not all of me—only my eyes; yes, my eyes rose up the entire Tree of Kabbalah, that great Tree of the ten sefiroth. My eyes rose up and beheld, in the distance, far beyond the Tree itself, an image of a fountain. Yet it was not a fountain. Water poured like a holy flame out of this fountain, yet one did not see the fountain itself. One saw only the pouring out of the water-flame.

My vision of the fountain vanished as abruptly as it had come to me. I was then left with a strange sense of futility and wonderment as to why I was vouchsafed this vision, only to have it taken away before I could learn anything, experience anything, or answer again—as I felt I must—the question, "Why six million dead Jews?"

The feeling of futility was worsened by a strange event in the world. A leading political figure from a great American family was shot by an assassin, just as the leader was enjoying a triumph in his campaign for high office. The family had been rent asunder by many deaths and agonies. Here, again, another rending asunder, and now by a dark little man, of whom one knew nothing, except that he was born in Jerusalem.

What was all this darkness, I asked myself? One felt the bleakness of the symbols of that poor family, Christ-like in the continual sacrifice of their innocent sons... And yet, and yet, what was all the violence and lawlessness about? "Violence and lawlessness—how awful," complained the nation, yet it was often violent and lawless itself. Was she, in secret, fascinated by the violence? Is that the evil?

Violence, death, lawlessness. Death, lawlessness, violence. I sank down under these and it seemed that I was now occupied with the part of the question, "Why six million dead Jews?" which had to do with death. DEATH. The word leaped out at me. It was larger now than dead Jews alone. There was a dead white hero and several dead black heroes. Why Death ? The question came in capital letters:

WHY DEATH? And now the word changed, and I saw, instead, the tetragrammaton, the holy name of God which the pious Jews of old never permitted themselves to pronounce: YHVH. Yahveh or Jehovah.

As I pronounced the sacred name, as I violated the ancient taboo, there appeared before me the image of a man strangely familiar to me. He had a dark beard, was clearly a Jew, and had a scholarly manner about him. I recognized him: he was none other than myself from a previous incarnation. I knew at once that I was faced with the Rabbi of myself of lifetimes centuries before. I intuited that I once again was going to play out the conflict between gypsy and Jew, between woman and man, between rationalist and mystic. But now the struggle would be within myself. I was going to have to solve for myself the conflict that had plagued me through many lives. How, indeed, could I be a medium for God, a creature meant to express the occult truths of the Most High, how could I do this if I could not even reconcile these differences within myself?

As I thought these thoughts, the Rabbi nodded. It was as if we both knew our long history of struggle, of how we had betrayed each other, of how we had hurt, fought, loved and were passionately tied to each other. I had been now one, now the other, sometimes experiencing the other in the form of another person, sometimes as myself. But now, dear Lord, now, in Thy Name, we were going to reconcile ourselves at last, if we could. And we were going to do this in answer to the question, "Why six million dead Jews?" For only between us, only in the union of passion and mind, female and male, could we hope for a solution.

The Rabbi then spoke:

"Death. Lawlessness. Violence. Evil. We must, you and I, struggle with the questions of Death, of the Law, and of Evil. For only then can we contribute our part in the answer to the QUESTION. For it is the Question that must be capitalized, as well as death and evil; the Lord must acknowledge the question, our question, the Jew's question, mankind's question. Let us begin Sophie-Sarah."

"Begin, then, Rabbi, Tell me what you know of Death. Why is there death in the world?"

"The Torah begins with God creating the world. He is, thus, a creator God. Did He, then, create the opposite of creation, did He create death? No. For the Torah says that it was man who created death. Our first parents created death by the sin of disobedience; they ate the fruit of the Tree of Knowledge. The Tree of Knowledge, therefore, is the same as the Tree of Death, just as we were told. Man was expelled from Paradise, kept away from the Tree of Life, from having immortality. Death, sayeth the Lord, comes from knowing, and particularly, from knowing how to distinguish good from evil. Man is to blame, therefore.

"My understanding of this, Sophie-Sarah, is that Death is a consequence of consciousness, of awareness of separation. Death, therefore, is partly an illusion. For we die, are reborn, die again. God originally meant us to be forever alive. And thus we are; though we must die and be reborn in order to achieve again, ultimately, the state for which we were meant. We are meant to 'be as Gods'."

"Rabbi, your words are too intellectual. Though they may be true, they carry no fire, they carry no weight. That same Lord who blamed man for the existence of Death also said, 'Thou shalt not kill.' Yet He kills more than anyone. The Lord is a slaughterer, or have you not read that in your Torah? The mind cannot speak of death. The mind can only speculate about it. The heart must speak."

"The heart may speak, Sophie-Sarah, but there must be understanding as well. I understand that the Lord needed our consciousness. I understand that the Lord let our first parents taste of that Tree of Knowledge, because He needed our understanding. He needed a consciousness to share creation with. Now that is not only dryness of the mind, is it?"

"No, Rabbi, it is not. What you say is true, but I must turn from you, oh Rabbi. I must turn from you when it comes to death. The heart must cry out to God for the death of the six million Jews. The heart must also cry out for the death of the fallen American Christian and his martyr brother, their parents and wives and children. The heart must cry out and speak, too, to the fallen black Americans and their parents and wives and children. For how can we explain to them, the close ones, the death of their loved ones? You, Rabbi, cannot. Nor can I.

"You, oh Lord, help us to explain to them! Tell us why the innocent die. Help us, we Jews who have suffered the innocent death of the Six Million, and the millions before in our history, help us to explain to the poor-rich white Christian family the personal tragic death of their sons, and to the black families who have had the same.

"What can we say to the twenty million black people who have suffered just as Jews have suffered? What can be said to them?... Nothing. For they will have to write a new Bible, and a new Word of the Lord.

"Well, then, Oh Lord, my God, speak to me from Your Holy Fire, tell me in words of the agony of the people, who wait, Oh Lord, in their pain of violence and rending asunder. Think Lord, even of Your instrument, the Arab assassin who foolishly took the hero's life, in the belief that he was a positive vehicle of his country! And think of the Arab's poor mother who can only weep!"

How long, O Lord? How long?

How long will we, suffering mankind, have to await redemption?

How long must we tolerate our own ignorance and pain, and have it compounded by Your own?

How long must we cope with our own violence and greed and horror, and also have to take on Your own?

Is there no end to it?

Is there no end to the burden that both we and You have put upon us?

There is no end, my son. There is no end.

You speak to me as Your Son. I am not Your Son. I am a woman, and true, and I cry out in anguish.

I will not bear Your burden like a loyal son, for I am a woman.

I am tempted to be a loving and understanding mother-daughter to You. But I will cry out.

All my creatures are as sons to me. Of this, too, there is no end. Of creation there is no end. Nor of destruction. I give and take away. And I am given and am taken away. The Christ is my son and I am he. The white is my son and I am he. The black is my son and I am he.

The mothers are my sons and they are me. All is I, and all is not I. Thus is my name called, "I am" for all that is, is "I am." In the beginning, there is the Lord "who." And that is the Lord "he" of "whom" you speak. Then, in the course of the aeons, there is the Lord "you," who spoke to Moses and to Buddha and to Christ. And now there will be the Lord "I" to whom even Sophie-Sarah will speak.

These words of God, these words of YHVH—for I was convinced that they came from the same source as had spoken to Abraham and Isaac and Jacob, and to Moses and David and Jesus—these words came slowly and heavily and quietly. There was no thunder in them. There was not even any fire in them. But they came as heavy chunks of rich earth, each of which had a tongue in it which could speak His name. For that is the *name* of God, too. The spirit speaks through the earth, the Voice of God speaks through his creatures in the flesh. And I, even I, Sophie-Sarah, the lowly handmaiden, will be the Lord God, "I" to whom He will speak as "You and I" as He did with Abraham and Isaac and Jacob and Moses and David, and even as an "I" as He was with Jesus. For now the Lord will speak through me as "I!"

It is too much, for it is like a psalm without being a poem. There is an answer to each part of the question: "Why Six Million dead Jews?" "Six Million" answered, and "Death" answered. Jews, those chosen ones, that too, has been answered. And now, the question "Why?" becomes replaced by the question "Who?" and the question "Who?" is replaced by a sequence of "He" to "You" to "I" The whole question is raised, and it is answered: Listen, oh Humankind, for the Lord, our God, the Lord is One!

IV

The heart had spoken when it came to the struggle with Death. And I was glad. For what can the mind do with death except rationalize or explain? It cannot take away the fear of death, or the pain to loved ones. Only the heart can endure that. But the heart needs the mind after all. I thought such thoughts some days after this numinous encounter with God, and I felt guilty. For I had abandoned the Rabbi of my soul, just after he had come to me. I was guilty of repeating once more the rejection and one-sidedness that I had done throughout my incarnations: heart or mind; passion or truth; mysticism or reason; never both. And now the heart had won. But had it really? Was not what the Rabbi had to say true? Were not his words about the task of man having to help God in His creation a deep and passionate truth? And was it not also true that man needs to be ready for this in order to grow up to it? I realized my error and came to my Rabbi asking for forgiveness from this holy man so recently found and so quickly rejected.

"Do not trouble yourself, Sophie-Sarah," he said. "I know that Death cannot be answered with reason alone. I know that understanding and logic are no match for fear and passion. But my words are not just logic. Indeed, there are those who would call me fool, call me one of faith, not reason. No matter. Our task is understanding, and to help the Lord come to greater consciousness of Himself. For this, the heart is needed, too. The mind bows to passion. Was it not a non-Jew who said, 'Let reason be a slave of the passions?' I agree. Let reason and understanding serve the flaming heart and fiery fountain which emerges from the God who is forever unmanifest. The limitless God, the *Ain Sof* who is beyond all words and images and ideas, is that fountainless fountain which you experienced when you reflected upon the QUESTION for the second time. It is from that source that the holy water-fire comes, and it is because of that fire in you that I bow to you. For reason is like the fountain, it must be the vessel and servant of the water-fire."

"Strange, Rabbi," said I. "You, a man, being a vessel for a woman. It is rather like the images I have heard of: the Jews are like a woman, married to God. They, too, are a vessel for His fire. I blush at the comparison, Rabbi. You swell me up, and I am in as great a danger of pride as our first parents!"

"Have no fear, Sophie-Sarah, we have more to do than can be managed by you or me alone—or, indeed, by you and me together. That stops pride. Let us continue with our task. We have faced Death. We must, yet, face Lawlessness and the Law. And for this, I must say, knowledge and the mind will need a place."

"It is true, Rabbi. Among the dreams I had, came the command, 'REINTERPRET THE LAW.' That, too, was a *mitzvah* from God, a commandment. Imagine! A commandment to reinterpret the Ten commandments, a law to re-interpret the law. I will surely need all that you can give for this task."

"Sophie-Sarah, you have struggled with the *gematria* of the numbers especially of the number six, just as did the old Kabbalists. Now you—and I—must struggle with the gematria of the *letters*. I must tell you that the old Kabbalists recognized the Voice of the Lord as the instrument of creation. The Voice of the Lord is the Law and it is expressed by the instrument of the Word. But the word is made up of letters, those twenty-two in Hebrew and twenty-six in English. When God speaks, he speaks in words, and the words are made of the twenty-two or twenty-six letters. Each creation is a word, the pious rabbis told us, and each exegesis of Torah rises up as a *mitzvah* and a creation. So, then, Sophie-Sarah, your *mitzvah* and commandment to re-interpret the law is a creation. The Voice commanded you to listen and think anew, thus create anew. And for this will I help you. Shall we reflect?"

"Rabbi, your words are like a clear stream which cools my fire and make me happy to be with you. Begin the clear stream of your questions and reflections. I shall accompany you as best I can. Thus, I pray, may I serve the *mitzvah* that God has given to me."

"What is 'The Law'?", the Rabbi began. "How are we to understand it? Is it the 'statutes' of God and His 'decisions' (*toroth*) ? Is it the written words of the entire Bible? Yes and no. For 'Law' is *Torah* which means 'oral direction.' God speaks in words and the words filter down and grow hardened into written statements and into 'laws' as statutes. But directions are not statutes, Sophie-Sarah. The Lord gave you a mitzvah (a direction, a command, a task, an oral law), no ordinary 'statute' such as most of the six-hundred-thirteen in the Bible which include such laws as a prohibition against wearing clothing made of linen and wool... And yet, 'The law is the law,' say the judges, secular and religious. For all laws, they imply, are the Word of God. It is so?"

"I do not think so, Rabbi," said I. "The laws may have been the word of God in the beginning, but when they harden into statutes, they are already dead. And deadly, rigid men use these statutes against us, to hurt our hearts and restrict our freedom."

"You speak of 'in the beginning,' Sophie-Sarah. In the beginning, we are told, was the Law of the Ten Commandments. God spoke to Moses and Moses spoke to the people. Moses brought the Ethical Code, but there was a Ritual Code, too. There were two stone tablets, were there not? Perhaps the ethical code was on one and the ritual code on the other. Are we obliged to follow all of the laws? All six-hundred-thirteen? If so, then the code, the law, becomes a meaningless burden, and where, then, do we have the Simchath Torah, joy in the law? I do not know, perhaps one must choose, Sophie-Sarah.

"There always have been those who followed the letter of the law and not the spirit. We don't need the Christians to tell us about that, do we? We have great Kabbalists who tell us that even the Torah itself, as written, is merely the Throne of God, the seat upon which He sits. The Voice of God is the reality; it is the unseen Voice which sits upon the Throne that we worship and obey. It is with Him that we dance in alacritous union like a joyous Chassid!"

"Now you speak my language, Rabbi! Voice of God and Throne of God; it is the Voice that we worship in dance. Yes."

"It is not just I, Sophie-Sarah, who speaks this way. Listen to Jeremiah about the law, for he, we are told by rabbinical tradition, was the guardian of the original Stones. After Moses and Noah, it was Jeremiah who kept the ark of the stones, until Jerusalem—blessed be her gorgeous memory—was taken by the tyrant Nebuchadnezzar.

"What does Jeremiah say of the Voice? Jeremiah said that the Lord told him: 'For in the day that I brought them out of the land of Egypt, I did not speak to your fathers or command them concerning burnt offerings and sacrifices. But this command I gave them, Obey My voice, and I will be your God, and ye shall be My people; and walk ye in all the ways that I have commanded you, that it may be well with you.' Thus sayeth Jeremiah.

"But it seems as if the Lord changed his mind," said I, "for earlier he lusted after sacrifices and burnt offerings."

"Yet again," The Rabbi continued, "Jeremiah tells us—nay, promises us—from the Lord: I will put my law in their inward parts, and write it in their hearts; and will be their God, and they shall be My people."

"Ah, would that this were true," I said, "that the law be written in our hearts and inward parts. If that were true, we would no longer need the wisdom of St. Paul who went beyond the law, through the law. Nor even Jesus, who came to fulfill the law, but transcended it into the one law of Love of God and neighbor.

"But the Sermon on the Mount did not accomplish it for Christians either. St. Paul spoke truly of them, as of himself and us, when he said that the law was not written in their flesh. So, then, oh God, what is Your law, that we struggle with it, obey it, defy it, violate it, interpret it, but do not find it, alas, in our hearts or inward parts? It does not touch our flesh."

Thus did I turn toward God, but no answer to my question came, so my Rabbi and I turned to the laws themselves, the basic ten as given us.

"The sages tell us," the Rabbi said, "that there is, in truth, only one law, that against idolatry. Adultery, after all, originally meant idolatry. God means, therefore, that we should really have no images of Him at all! We must hear His Voice and break all idols, including the images of Him which become outworn. He, Blessed be His Holy Name, will not be contained in any images, or idols, or symbols. He, the Silent One, the Transcendent One, will go beyond all of them. This is His Voice and His Commandment, and that, we need to know, is not a burden but a *mitzvah*, a joyous fact of eternity!"

"I agree, Rabbi. The voice is forever. The throne must be renewed!"

"But let us look at the laws, Sophie-Sarah. Perhaps we can then understand the voice from the shape of the throne."

"Yes, Rabbi, you are right."

"The first few laws," the Rabbi said, "speak mostly of God Himself, and His vanity. No other Gods, no images, no taking the Name in vain. Enjoining us to copy His creativity, including the Sabbath, for Him. He even tells us that He is a jealous God... I start to understand. Jealousy, vanity, changing His mind; it sounds more like a powerful and intense woman, not a man!

"Rabbi!" I said. "No wonder He called me Son, I called him Father! God is a jealous female, demanding and vain, like many of us!

"God is a Goddess! And the Laws which are trying to be expressed by Him-Her are the Laws of His-Her nature, not ordinary statutes which we enact as a convenience and then discard."

"I begin to glimpse what is meant, Rabbi. Thou shalt not commit adultery—not adulterate and water down. Thou shalt love totally. And who, pray, but a woman could command love? 'Thou shalt love the Lord, thy God, with all thine heart and with all thy soul and with all thy might.' As if love can be commanded at all! Yet it is true, as a natural law, is it not? That thou shalt love whether thou knowest it or not, likest it or not, it will show itself some way. Some men worship power and that is their love, their God. Others love fame or fortune, or lust, or self. The chief value is God, and that is always loved totally, is it not? The Lord is telling us, in Torah, that His laws are the Laws of the Soul. They, our people, comprehended it at that level then, and we must, all of us, understand it anew."

"You are right, Sophie-Sarah," said the Rabbi. "We have had science, but no real science of the soul. Religion speaks to the soul and we must find the laws of the soul. Perhaps the laws of the soul are the laws of nature in microcosm. Is the Goddess speaking, telling us of Her Nature?"

"I think so, Rabbi."

"Ah, Sophie-Sarah, you are starting to think. Just as I bowed to heart and soul, you begin to think. Perhaps we will merge in the law, the laws of the Goddess, no less, and become as one.

"But I want to return to the Stones, the Tablets of the Law. I want, still, to understand the Law, before I merge with it. The Ten Commandments, scholars tell us, were really called the Ten Words. TEN WORDS. What could this mean, or could it have meant? Was not God telling Moses of His-Her Nature? Were these not the Ten Names of God as the Kabbalists tell us, in the Tree of the Ten Sefiroth? Thus it seems to me. For God is always speaking to us in His Voice, and we can comprehend it only in part. We codify and enclose it, in order to keep it—bless our poor, bumbling hearts—but we fail. We must listen anew to the Voice, to the Ten Words, the Ten Names of God, and hear again what His/Her nature is, and how we are to understand it.

"For that is the Law: That thou shalt love with all thy might and heart and soul. With total devotion, always. There is nothing else that can be done, you can hardly do otherwise. All you can do is better understand, better worship that which you love and adore and serve. And you had best grow more conscious of it, lest you worship a stone idol, a dead image! Praise the Lord; Blessed be His-Her Name!"

"Beautiful, Rabbi" I said. "You are speaking, now, with a heart. Let us speak the Ten Words, the Ten Names of God, and see what feelings, what images they evoke. Let us speak the names of the Lord, as the Kabbalists have given them to us."

"Hear, first, Sophie-Sarah," said my beloved Rabbi, "the great Rabbi Eleazar, who sings, in the Kabbalistic Zohar, with an audacity greater than ours:

> Before God created the world, His name was enclosed within Him, and therefore He and His name enclosed within Him were not one. Nor could this unity be effected until He created the world... He made it for His own behoof, for His own advantage, to display His glory, to show that He is one and His name is one.

"So, do you see, Sophie-Sarah? Rabbi Eleazar knew, long ago, as we know, that God created the world and the Law for His benefit, to be united with His Name, His holy Oneness. So, to know His Law, we need to know His Name! That is the Law! Hear further what good Rabbi Eleazar says:

> 'And the earth was void and without form.' This describes the original state—as it were, the dregs of ink clinging to the point of the pen—in which there was no subsistence, until the world was graven with forty-two letters, all of which are the ornamentation of the Holy Name. When they are joined, letters ascend and descend, and form crowns for themselves in all four quarters of the world, so that the world is established through them and they through it.

"So, my Lord; let us, Sophie-Sarah and I, establish Your Name. Let the crowns of our saying Your Name arise, and allow You to unite with Yourself. Our saying thereof unites You with Your Shekhinah, and thus the King is reunited with the Crown. Thus do we follow and meditate upon God's law."

Thus did my Rabbi speak knowingly and beautifully. And thus did our meditation begin. Hear, now, our meditation upon the Law, the Words, the Names of God.

"In the beginning," the Rabbi began, "before there appears even the Name, or the thought of the Name, is the *Ain Sof*, beyond the limitless All. And then a breath occurs and the Holy Name makes itself manifest, as the 'supreme crown.' But this supreme crown of God carries the Name (whisper it, do not shout it) EHYEH. And what is this EHYEH? What does it mean? It means only 'I shall be.' Oh, Great Lord, what a great Name is this; for the Lord sayeth to Himself, as the 'He' 'Who' knew Himself and proclaimed His state of creating Himself: 'I begin with a future!' What great name of the Lord is this? 'I shall be'—EHYEH. So, in the beginning, when the breath moved in a whisper, the great 'I AM' stated His intention, His being and the fact, 'I shall be.' Thus is the Name of the Lord. For ever and ever: EHYEH 'Time is created out of timelessness.'

"The Crown, and 'I shall be.' Beautiful God pours Himself like an upside down crown from heaven. The King abandons His rulership and pours out His holy water-fire toward creation. I feel it, Rabbi. I feel that when God proclaims His Name, EHYEH, He has already proclaimed that I, even I, Sophie-Sarah, shall exist as well. EHYEH, Time and Being come into existence. Yes, Rabbi, beautiful."

"The Name of the Lord moved onward," continued the Rabbi. "Now came the name, ASHER, and the fuller name, ASHER EHYEH. And what, pray tell, does the Lord mean with this name ASHER? Blessed be His Name, ASHER means only 'which.' Imagine. We have had 'Who,' 'He,' 'You,' 'I am' as Names of God, and now we have 'I shall be which.' Particulars are formed in time. In ASHER, the Lord is a point. At that particular moment in the time of the beginning, the Lord particularizes: He curls up upon Himself, and can say only that He is a point. But, the Rabbis tell us, ASHER is also the mystic and recondite temple, the source of the 'beginning,' of Reshith. It is the point of Wisdom, the primordial intelligence of God. That, we know, comes from *Rosh*, the head. Rosh, anagramatically, comes from the letters of ASHER, Aleph, Shin, and Resh. So, ASHER is the 'which,' which is the beginning, the idea, the head and point and source."

"Rabbi," I said. "The *gematria* of the letters of the names of God are too puzzling to me. I can only understand ASHER as particular, individual—that I can comprehend and treasure. That God curled up upon Himself, like a caterpillar about to nest, and then transformed Himself into a butterfly, that I understand. The play with the letters I leave to you, Rabbi. God like a caterpillar, a unique and particular caterpillar, undergoing transformation into a whole new state—that is enough for me."

"From the 'beginning' in wisdom," the Rabbi went on, "the Name, hidden and mysterious, moves on, out of the temple palace, into the creative mystery of the *Bara Shith*, the 'beginning' in fact: 'He created six' on the sixth day. He created the six directions and, wonder of wonders, Man! Now, the seed comes to light. The Zohar, the bright splendor, inches its way and we come beyond the primordial idea of ASHER; we come to intelligent understanding and the expression of God in the Voice. For now we have the Voice of the Shofar, the ram's horn.

"This Voice of the Shofar announces, on the Day of Atonement, that God is also in the state of at-one-ment. What is this Atonement, this unity, this complete blending of the 'upper waters' and the 'lower waters?' Of Heaven above, and Earth below? Of the created universe with the mind of

God? It is none other than the One, unspeakable NAME—the one NAME which we Jews are not allowed to utter, the Name YHVH. And why are we not allowed to utter it? Is it because this tetragrammaton is just the 'not speakable,' and 'limitless?' No, because we already have this Name of God, in the Ain Sof. And that is quite 'speakable' for we have no strictures against it. Is it, then, because if we speak it, we are, like some primitive, stepping upon the shadow of God, and that makes Him nervous and irritable? Certainly not.

"The truth, Sophie-Sarah, is that when we speak the Name YHVH, we are entering into the primordial creative act itself! This tetragrammaton has an intimate connection with the primordial Thought: For IT, the tetragrammaton, the fourfold Word, was the chosen instrument for making the Divine Thought intelligible and realizable to the human mind. The Divine Name was enclosed within the Lord, and the very speaking of the NAME was one of the purposes of creation. So, when we see or speak the Name YHVH we are participating in the Divine Creation itself!"

"Rabbi, that the shofar, the sound of the ram's horn should announce God's union with His Name, His at-one-ment, and ours with Him; and that the six is the number of creation, those two things I glimpse intuitively. For it is true that in creation I am at one with God, and like a God. When I gave birth to my children, I felt like both a handmaid of God, and a Goddess myself. I also understand unspeakableness. I understand that there is that which cannot be spoken, should one desire it or not. Every woman understands the wordless look of love. But I still do not understand your *gematria*, Rabbi. Explain to me, for I would understand with the head, the *Rosh*, as you say, as well as with the heart."

"Each letter of the Holy Name, Sophie-Sarah, is associated with a separate grade of creation. Thus, with the grade *Reshith*, the 'beginning', there is the letter Yod. With the next grade, *Elohim Hayyim* (the Lord creating the Heavens), there is the letter He. This He is the 'upper He' of the creation of the Heavens, and these heavens are of the letter Vau. Now we come to the 'second He,' the 'lower He,' and this is the creation of the earth. For, 'In the beginning, the Lord God created the Heaven and the Earth.' And these are the letters of the Name of God, YHVH. On the first day, there existed the creation of the letters Yod and He; with the second day, the combination of Vau and He; while with the third day all four letters were combined into YHVH. This is the making manifest, the transformation of YHVH, the unspeakable, into JEHOVAH, the speakable name of God."

"Rabbi, dear Rabbi. Your Gematria escapes me. You go too far from images. I feel that I am being lectured at, rather than being with a beloved friend who is meditating with me. I have read Kabbalah, too, dear Rabbi, and I particularly like what Rabbi Hiya said about the process of making manifest, about the time when the voice of YHVH is heard. Probably you know the quotation I mean. He was speaking about the passage in Torah when:

> The flowers appear on the earth, the time of song is come, And the voice of the turtle is heard in our land.

"Rabbi Hiya said that when God created the world, He endowed it with everything, but only in potential. When, however, man appeared, forthwith 'the flowers appeared on the earth'—all the latent powers were revealed. 'The time of song was come': the earth was now ripe to offer up praises to the Almighty, which it could not do before man was created. 'And the voice of the turtle is heard in our land': this is the word of God, of YHVH, which was not in the world till man was created."

"That is beautiful, Sophie-Sarah. I bow to the wisdom and beauty of Rabbi Hiya. But I bow even deeper to the poetry of The Book, the poetry which speaks of the voice of God as the turtle's voice.

"This turtle song, this sweet silent voice which sings in Spring, the time of creation, the day of creation of man. For does the turtle not have six points: four feet, head and tail? Does he not have an upper shell and lower shell, like the letter, He's, in YHVH? Do not the shells have hexagrams upon them? And do not the roundness of the shells speak of the point and circle of the first beginnings? Yes, Sophie-Sarah, the 'voice of the turtle' is the Voice of God.

"What remains to be said after this? Nothing. What more can one say after one has invoked the Divine Voice of the turtle? Nothing. What more can one do than sing the praises of the Almighty in YHVH? Nothing... Yet, but yet, the NAMES of the Divine One, blessed be He, go on, for now we have touched only three of the Divine ten and we must go on and speak of the other seven and thus arrive at the totality of the TEN. This is our mitzvah, and commandment, Sophie-Sarah, for of the Commandments and of the NAMES, there are ten."

"Let us go on, Rabbi."

"After YHVH, there is EL GADOL, the 'Great God.' The Great God is that which emerged from the primal ether, and that is the great God of light. For the Lord said, 'Let there be light' and it was this Name of the Lord, EL GADOL, which emerged with the lightness, as the lightness of the sun. But it was not our sun; it was the primordial sun, the sun of consciousness which was long before the light of the sun. Oh, EL GADOL, primordial Lord of Light, Who said 'Let there be...' With the light, there came, also, kindness, and the love of God, which is warm and compassionate, yielding and merciful. All this was on the Right side.

"At the same moment, at the second day of the creation, came the Left side, the power and stern judgment and punishment of God, and the Name of ELOHIM. With ELOHIM, there came also Darkness, thus sayeth the

Lord. Thus created He, them. For the 'Them' is the disunity, the 'many' of ELOHIM. Sh-sh-sh. God is also a plurality! ELOHIM is the name of God having to do with the 'more,' the angels and the powers. Even good Rabbi Simeon, he of the benevolent wisdom of Zohar, tells us that the angels are jealous of man! Mind you, the angels of God, yea, even the parts of God, are jealous of man. Did not the Lord tell us that He is a jealous God? Yes, for thus is He a plurality, jealous of other Gods. 'No other Gods before me.' He is like a woman, and dark, with her dark face of passion—jealous."

"Rabbi, perhaps the trouble in understanding lies with me. I understand your Lord of Light, the sun; I grasp the plurality of Elohim, the darkness; I sense, too, the struggle of Right and Left, of kindness and mercy versus jealousy and judgment. But I only sense and understand, Rabbi, I do not feel. Make me feel, Rabbi! Make me know in my flesh these names of God, EL GADOL and ELOHIM. Were not these names and laws to be written and felt in the flesh?"

"Oh, Sophie-Sarah! You do not need my words for it, for the understanding of it, for the grasping of it. Has not your life and my life been just such a struggle between mercy and judgment, giving and getting? Have you not suffered the conflict between the one God and the many, the one love and the many? Have not jealousy and desire clawed your being? This battle within God is the battle of our deepest selves and you know it. You know, too, that beyond EL GADOL and ELOHIM, beyond the battle of light and dark, of the one and the many, of love and power, there is reconciliation in the name of JEHOVAH, of YHVH made manifest in compassion and beauty. For here, the voice of the turtle is heard in mercy and sweetness."

"You are right, Rabbi. I knew this, but I suppose that I needed you to remind me of it. I needed, perhaps, to know that you, too, knew it, in your bones and heart, and not only with your head. Our lives, indeed, are of the Lord, right and left, light and dark, one and many, EL GADOL and ELOHIM."

"The 'small still voice' which comes after the fire," continued the Rabbi, the sweet voice of YHVH as it manifests in JEHOVAH, lasts only for a time, and the next NAMES of the Lord bring quaking and fear and chaos. What are these NAMES? They are ZEBAOTH and SHADDAI. ZEBAOTH, the Lord of Hosts, the martial God, the God of spirits who instills fear into the hearts of Israel's enemies! This is the NAME which is the author of the *Bohu*, the 'quaking' of the *Tohu-Bohu*, the chaos and the quaking. Just as Darkness was under the aegis of ELOHIM, and spirit under the aegis of YHVH, then Bohu, the quaking, is under the martial lord of ZEBAOTH, and chaos under the mystic nature of SHADDAI.

"Further, beyond the battling of the Lord, beyond the chaos and quaking of the mystic nature, beyond the Lord of Hosts and the Lord of Chaos, comes the reconciliation, once again, in the EL. EL is the 'Glory of

God.' This is God when He is manifest in His Glory, a glory, as Rabbi Simeon tells us, which is splendor upon splendor, when the 'heavens declare the glory of God' as her bridegroom. For this EL manifests when there is a union of God with His Own Glory. God is united with Himself, and this is the basis and foundation of all the active forces in the Lord. Here is another *gematria* of letters: EL (the great God, in His Glory), combined with H and Y and M to form in our Hebrew tongue, ELOHIM. And the He, Yod, Mim, with which the El combined, make *hayam*, the sea, and the lower waters. The 'upper waters' combine with the 'lower waters' in the great unity of the Lord. This is the meaning of the upper He and the lower He."

"Enough of Gematria, Rabbi. And enough, too, of ZEBAOTH and SHADDAI. Enough of wars, enough of battles, enough of fear. We can bow to EL, God's glory, without such chaos and quaking."

"Oh, Sophie-Sarah, it is because of the chaos and the quaking that we must resort to gematria! Without our poor attempts at trying to understand, without our efforts after divining the meaning, the direction of God's will, without those, well then, the Power of God, especially when it is frightening and destructive, would break our poor heads!"

"Just, Rabbi, as God's love can break our poor hearts! I understand, Rabbi, I understand."

"Let us go beyond the nine Names, Sophie-Sarah. Let us complete our *mitzvah* and task. Let us go beyond the nine to the tenth.

"Could there be more than this nine-fold unity of the Names of the Lord? Of course, for the Nine are as nothing without the tenth, and the tenth is ADONAI, the Lord of Earth. What is the Lord without His creation, the earth? Nothing, or nearly nothing, for without His creation there would be no one to sing the praises of the Lord, to exult in His creation, and to reflect upon the Glory and help the Lord unite with his Shekhinah! Sophie-Sarah, that is the whole work of the Universe: to assist the Supreme Crown of the Lord to unite with His Kingdom and become the Lord of the Earth, ADONAI. The Lord of the Heavens, of the supreme crown, is incomplete without his Kingship, and this Kingdom is that of Mankind."

"Amen, Rabbi, amen. Now I understand you. Now I am with you."

"Rabbi Eleazar tells us that Adon (Lord) is another name of the ark of the covenant. So, ADONAI, the Lord of the Covenant, is the One Lord who made a Covenant with His people, Israel, and through His people, with Mankind. ADONAI, thus, is the LORD of the Covenant, of God contacting and binding Himself with His creation, the people, and thus coming to His own union.

"It is written: 'The Lord reigneth, the Lord hath reigned, the Lord will reign for evermore.' There is an upper world and a lower world, the upper being a pattern for the lower. The Lord reigneth above, the Lord reigneth in the middle: these are the 'reignings' of the first nine names. 'The Lord will reign below' is the Lord ADONAI, the tenth name. It is He who made the sign of the covenant, and remakes His sign again and again. Each time, His covenant is more of Himself. Praised be ADONAI!

"At one time, King David reversed the order, Rabbi Aha tells us, and said: 'The Lord is King for ever and ever,' thus in a psalm. 'The Lord is king,' below, 'for ever' in the middle, 'and ever,' above, for there is the reunion and perfection of all. God 'is king' above, and 'will reign' below.

"So, praised be ADONAI, the Lord of earth, where the Crown unites with the King. The King without a crown is the Lord without his *Shekhinah*. Mankind without the Lord is the Kingdom without its King! *Shema Yisrael Adonai Elohenu, Adonai Echod!* Hear, Oh Israel, the Lord our God, the Lord is One.

"Thus are the Ten Commandments: the ten NAMES of the One God. And that is the law; to utter His Name, in creation, in love!"

"Thus did the Rabbi and I complete our meditation upon the Ten Names of God, the Ten Laws of God, and the goal of God."

V

Many months passed before I could again address myself to the question of "Why six million dead Jews?" Indeed, I had hoped that perhaps I was freed of the questionable blessing, of the *mitzvah* which I had received to cope with that problem. Just as he had appeared, the Rabbi of my soul had vanished after we had accomplished our meditation upon the Names of the Lord. Though I missed him a little, I counted it a blessing, I must confess, to go about my daily life, and live simply and accept whatever joy came my way. If that constituted a running away from the "commandment," let it be so—I ran. For, despite the greatness of the Lord's Voice, despite the wonder of His communication, I knew what it meant to "fear God." I was reminded of the first precept of Rabbi Simeon in the Zohar.

Rabbi Simeon knew that the real fear of God was not the fear that one may lose family or possessions, nor the fear that one will suffer punishment and tortures of Gehenna; no, not these. The real fear is the anxiety before the Master, blessed be He, who exists. That is the fear before the *tremendum*, the holy fear, which is neither fear of the lash nor of the loss, but fear of the Lord! This is the fear, the Torah tells us, which is the beginning of wisdom.

I also understood Rabbi Simeon's second precept that one does not love God merely because He has provided one with riches, or length of life, or children, or power over enemies. No, none of these. Does one still love the Lord when one is poor, or childless or weak? Can one still love the Holy One, blessed be He, should the wheel of fortune turn against him? This kind of love is the "great love," the perfect love.

I was beginning to know both perfect fear and perfect love. I whisper it, lest the Tempter, cursed be He, induce me into the sin of pride, of knowing too much. But that crinkle, that chink in my armor of satisfaction in everyday life would come up to haunt me of an evening. The darkness would creep upon me; depression and anxiety would vaguely haunt me. Still I turned away from these.

After some months, however, I could not turn away from what began to emerge in my dreams and then in my waking life. I experienced, in short, the haunting of the six million.

At first, I would hear only moaning and sighing in my dreams. Then there came louder cries and shouts and the calling of my name. Finally there came the Command, from the dead, from the six million, to speak to them of evil. "Why evil?" they shouted; "Why suffering?" they called.

"Have I not answered?" I dared to respond. "Did I not speak, from Kabbalah and from visions, in answer to the question, 'Why six million dead Jews?'"

"You have answered," one suffering soul said. "You have answered the question of the six, of the six million, of the six million dead, of the six million dead Jews, you have answered; but the question of evil, why evil, that you have not."

I paused. I thought. They wanted an answer, these dead, as the whole world wants an answer, as it has always wanted an answer. Is there an answer? I do not know. But I must answer; it is my mitzvah.

But I could not answer alone. I needed the help of my Rabbi, my Kabbalistic soul-brother whom I had neglectfully abandoned. No sooner had I acknowledged my need for his assistance, no sooner had I whispered, lovingly, "Rabbi," than he appeared, handsome and clear-eyed as before.

"Your need is my need, Sophie-Sarah," he said. "And your commandment is mine. How can we really be parted for long? Head without heart is like a dry river bed, a vessel without its cooling, nourishing stream."

"Yes, Rabbi," I said. "And heart without head is a raging fire with no chimney to direct its force to heaven, and no hearth to contain its warmth and show its gorgeous flame. We need each other."

"Let us try, then, Sophie-Sarah, to answer about evil. But now the commandment comes not from the Lord, but from the dead, those honored and despised, those terrible and beautiful dead."

"Yes, let us try, Rabbi. Help me, as I shall try to help you. Help me, first, with your mind and your knowledge. Help me speak of evil to the dead."

"Oh, dear dead," I, Sophie-Sarah, began. "I cannot answer, for I do not know the answer, but my Rabbi can tell you the answers of the Rabbis, blessed be their pure hearts, and of the scholars, blessed be their pure minds. My Rabbi knows much."

The dead left off their moaning. I trusted that they wanted his answer, so I turned to him, and he spoke:

"Evil, dear dead," began the Rabbi, "is separation, or isolation. Sin always destroys a union and this was the Original Sin, through which the fruit was separated from the tree, as one Rabbi puts it, or as Rabbi Ezra ben Solomon has proclaimed, when the Tree of Life was separated from the Tree of Knowledge. When a man falls into isolation, when he seeks to maintain his own self, his own pride, instead of the original context and harmony of all which has been created, then he has used the magic of the serpent. He has used this magic either to rend asunder God's order or to unite that which God has separated. That is evil.

"Thus, sayeth the Rabbis, Adam's sin was great. But Rabbi ben Yohai says that the *Sefiroth* were revealed to Adam in the shape of the Tree of Life and the Tree of Knowledge, in the form of the middle and last *Sefirah*. Adam, instead of preserving their original unity and thereby saving the wholeness of 'life' and 'knowledge' and bringing salvation to the world, separated the one from the other. Furthermore, Adam worshipped only the Shekhinah, the last *Sefirah*, and did not recognize its union with the other nine Sefiroth. Thus Adam interrupted the stream of life which flows from sphere to sphere and brought separation and isolation into the world. That is evil.

"So, from the beginning, with Adam, there has been a painful fissure, a rent, in the life and action of the Divine. This is the painful 'exile of the Shekhina.' Only when the original harmony is restored, as in the beginning, will 'God be one, and His name one,' for all time.

"Rabbi Simeon even says, 'It is therefore necessary for man to acknowledge that God and the Lord are one and the same without any cleavage whatever. The Lord He is God. When mankind will universally acknowledge this absolute unity, the evil power itself will be removed from the world and exercise no more influence upon earth.'

"How does man do this? How does he mend the rending? By religious acts: Torah, *mitzvoth*, and prayer. That extinction of the rending, of the stain, the restoration of harmony, that is the *tikkun*, man's task in the world. When all is redeemed, then 'there shall be perfection above and below, and all worlds shall be united in one bond.'"

As my Rabbi told these truths to the six million, as he explained the problem of man's sin and his task, and of the division in the Divine Life, they all nodded. They crossed their arms across their chests and took upon themselves the sin of our ancestor, for they knew, as we all knew, that all our souls were present at that first event, and that we all partook of Adam's sin of division.

"But," I, Sophie-Sarah, called out to them, my six million dead brothers and sisters, "our sin is also God's sin!"

They looked at me in amazement and fear. I was somewhat surprised, for my Rabbi and I had already hinted rather strongly at this viewpoint earlier, had we not? When we meditated upon the commandments and the NAMES of God? When we spoke of the necessity of God becoming human? Yes. But somehow, stating it so baldly was shocking. Not even the Zoharic Rabbis were so audacious. Was I not in danger of repeating Adam's sin? Perhaps. Let my Rabbi help me then, and return to what the learned scholars, and the pious Rabbis have said, for they, even they, tell us dark facts.

"The causes of evil lie deeper than human sin and pride and separation," continued my Rabbi. "No, Sophie-Sarah, evil was not created only by man—that would be an even greater *chutzpah*, to believe that! Even though the Torah hints at this, there are deeper truths from God—when one is ready to receive them. Nor is evil only, as some say, a relative matter, a figment of one's imagination. No, evil is real and exists—listen deeply, dearly beloved Sophie-Sarah and fellow Jews—in the nature of the Godhead Himself! There, one has said it. But one must explain:

"The totality of divine potencies, of the ten NAMES of God, and of the ten Sefiroth, is sacred and good, so long as each stays in relation to all the others. But the fundamental cause of evil, dearly beloved, is in *Geburah* and *Din*, the Power of God, the Sefirah of God's strict justice, rigor and judgment, as well as His power. When God's *Left Hand*, which symbolizes this *Sefirah*, is balanced by His Right Hand, the *Sefirah* of *Hesed*, of mercy and love, then all is order and good. Fierce fire, stern judgment, sacred wrath, must be balanced by mercy and love. But, dearly beloved, when the fierce fire of God, the stern judgment and sacred wrath tears itself loose, when it hypertrophies and breaks away from mercy, then, dear ones, the fire breaks away from God altogether and is transformed into Gehenna, and the dark world of Satan.

"Satan, the evil one, is the HYPERTROPHY OF GOD'S WRATH. So taught Moses de Leon, so taught the Zohar, and so, too, do I believe. Thus, dear friends, evil is from the Godhead Himself."

"Is it only you who thinks so, Rabbi? Now I, even I, Sophie-Sarah, would want other rabbinical authority for such a dangerous statement. I can imagine what the rabbi in my nice, American temple would do with such a statement! 'Evil is in the nature of the Godhead Himself'—our local rabbi would burst! Give us, Rabbi of my soul, give the dead and me other authorities for this view, please!"

"All right, Sophie-Sarah, let us hear the words of the good Rabbis. They, too, tell us that evil is from division. Division was created by God on the Second Day. Hear Rabbi Simeon:

"'And God said, Let there be a firmament in the midst of the waters. Here in the particular (day) there is an allusion to the separation of the upper from the lower waters, through that which is called 'the left.' Here, too, discord was created through that which is called 'the left.' For up to this point the text has alluded to the 'right'... It is in the nature of the right to harmonize the whole and, therefore, the whole is written with the right, since it is the source of harmony. When the Left awoke, there awoke discord, and through that discord, the wrathful fire was reinforced and there emerged the Gehinnom, which thus originated from the left and continues there.'

"Rabbi Simeon goes on to tell us how Moses tried to reconcile this division, but was only partly successful. The good Simeon continues: 'When discord was stirred by violence of the left, the Avenging Spirit was reinforced. There issued from it two demons which immediately became solidified without any moisture, one male and one female. From them were propagated legions of demons, and to this is due the inveteracy of the unclean spirit in all those demons. It is they who are symbolized by the foreskin; the one is called "adder" and the other is called "serpent," the two however being but one.'

"Do we not see, Sophie-Sarah and fellow Jews? The demons are 'without moisture,' no soft dew of kindness, no salty tears of love and wisdom, but dry as a desert. And the foreskin, that source of the demonic: Is it only the sensual which is so dark? No, for Rabbi Simeon goes on to speak of King Solomon—and who, Sophie-Sarah, is more sensual than King Solomon, he who sang in the Song of Songs? None. What does Rabbi Simeon say? He says:

"King Solomon, when he "penetrated into the depths of the nut garden," took a nut-shell (*klifah*) and drew an analogy from its layers to these spirits which inspire sensual desires in human beings, as it is written, "and the delights of the sons of men (are from) male and female demons..." The Holy One, Blessed be He, found it necessary to create all these things in the world to ensure its permanence, so that there should be, as it were, a brain with many membranes encircling it. The whole world is constructed on this principle, upper and lower from the first mystic point to the further removed of all the stages. They are all coverings one to another, brain within brain and spirit within spirit, so that one is a shell to another.'

"It is a great chain of being," my Rabbi continued with his own thought, "where everything is shell to a previous grade of perfection. And even the demonic is necessary to 'insure permanence' Can there be a nut without a shell? A brain without a membrane? Is not God a living Being?

"Even as the tree cannot exist without its bark, and the human body must shed its unclean sweat and blood, so does the demonic have its root in the mystery of God.

"More: The sensual is not the demonic, for the very union of God with his *Shekhinah* is sensual. It is the lower without the upper, the division of flesh and spirit, separation of soul and flesh—that is the evil.

"One thing more, Sophie-Sarah, one thing more, honored dead, and I will leave off my explanations, my quotations from authorities. The one thing more is to understand how it was that evil came into the world. How did evil begin? Evil began because the word *meoroth* (lights) is written defectively in Torah! When God says, Let there be lights in the firmament of the heaven to light upon the earth, 'lights' is defective. Rabbi Jose says: 'The defective spelling indicates the lowest, namely, the moon, which is the cause of the croup in children. It is also the cause of other misfortunes, because it is the smallest of all the luminaries, and sometimes it is obscured and receives no light at all.'

"Thus, dearly beloved, we are told that the 'lack of light' is the source of death, evil, Lilith. Lack of light. Lack of awareness, of consciousness. With this there is one-sided wrath and judgment. With this there is one-sided love. Not enough light. And it was so, in the beginning, on the second day, when discord was created. Listen now to Rabbi Isaac:

"'On the second day was created *Gehinnom* for sinners; on the second day, too, was created conflict. On the second day the work begun was not finished, and therefore the words "and it was good" are not used in connection with it. Not 'til the third day was the work of the second finished; hence in the account of that day we find twice the expression "that it was good," once in reference to its own proper work, and once in reference to the second day. On the third day, the deficiency of the second day was made good: discord was removed from it, and mercy was extended to the sinners in *Gehinnom*, the flames of which were moderated. Hence the second day is embraced in and completed by the third.'

"And those, oh six million, and Sophie-Sarah, those are the reasons for evil in the world."

As my Rabbi completed his explanation and his dissertation upon the reasons for evil in the world, I, Sophie-Sarah, turned to the dead, those six million who had haunted me with the question. I turned to them to see if this wise and profound answer satisfied them. As I looked, I thought I saw a smile. Can you imagine it? I thought I saw smiles upon the faces of those six million innocents who had suffered more, been tormented more, hounded more than any six million in history. But they smiled. They smiled and looked at me as if to ask, Was I satisfied with the answer of the Rabbi? They smiled as if to say that each and every one of them had his own experience of evil, his own explanation of evil, his own struggle with evil. Their struggles with evil, it was implied, was their own struggle with God. And no one can answer this question for anyone else! We can help each other, explain, just as my good Soul Rabbi had done, but each of us is ultimately alone with God and with the question of evil. Each must ask of God and answer to God about evil in Man and God... Thus did I understand, in a wordless, unspeakable way, what the honored dead, the tormented six million, were asking of me. And I knew that they were right.

I turned, therefore, to my Rabbi, and wondered if he, too, saw what I saw upon the faces of the six million. I wondered if he, too, was satisfied with his answers, the answers about evil from the Kabbalistic rabbis and from himself. I saw his face and that he, too, smiled. I saw that he, too, understood what I had understood from the dead. I saw that he, like me, could not only not answer for anyone else, that we cannot even answer for ourselves; that our lives are a struggle with God, to both give and get the answer to the problem of evil. Life is the answer.

But not only life is the answer, but love. For life without love is a life without union, and division is the evil. So, without further words, my Rabbi and I embraced. We joined hands and hearts and minds. We joined in a spiritual-soul-physical union where two became one. We joined in love and helped in our *Tikkun*, we helped assuage the evil in the world. Two became one, and I became whole.

VI

After my union with the Rabbi of my soul, after my vision of wholeness, I thought: I have answered enough. I have given the answers of the wise ones, of the Kabbalists, of the scholars, of the rabbis, and of God as He has spoken to me, Himself. It is enough, the NAMES, the *gematria* of the letters, the Law, the vision of the Evil One, himself. It is enough, it is enough, it is enough. Hound me no more, Oh Lord! Hound me no more, Oh Six Million! Thus did I think, in quietness and seclusion. So wise and secluded was I that I did not even withdraw, but lived my daily life as one should. Thankful are we for ritual; thankful are we for the strictures, the lines and the rules, which protect one from the living face of God.

Thus it was that I knew that I was protected from the Face of the Living God. And thus it was that I knew, that I, poor fool, thought I was preaching to the six million! Oh, now I knew in an instant that I was a fool! For it was not I but the Six Million who had seen the Living Face of God. They, dear Lord, have seen Your Face. They, dear Lord, have seen the darkest Face of all, and now they bask in the warmth of Your light Face, the face of Love and Care, like tender balls of cotton which soothe their wounds and rest their bones. The children dance about You and play at the feet of Your throne.

And what else, having seen Your darkest face? Man can only flee from Your face to Your face.

And I? I thought I was called to preach, to lecture, and to prophesy. For I am a Medium, am I not? Am I not the Medium, Sophie-Sarah? Am I not the chosen one of God, to speak of His message? Have I not been asked to speak for the Six Million?

I laugh. For He has spoken already to us all, and has shown His face to the Six Million. But not to me. Not to me. Show me Your face, dear Lord. Show me Your face. Speak to me. Break Your silence. Tell me. Tell me.

Not in the words I have used; no, not in those. But tell me, and show me. Until I am at rest, and, dear Lord, until You are at rest, too.

This was my prayer over time. It was a silent prayer as I went about my daily life. I said nothing. I went to *shul* and was a woman in *shul* like all others, listening, gossiping, praying. Accepting, from without, that this was a man's religion. But inside, but inside, I knew differently. I knew that it would change. I knew that we women would no longer sit only outside, or enclosed, or removed. For the face of God was going to be seen. And it, dear God, would be a feminine face, too.

So, I waited.

Time went by, and I did not know how to say it, do it, finish it, proclaim it. I had prayed, there was no answer. I had called out, but there was no statement in return... Again I laughed. Was this not the experience of the Six Million? Did they not call out, and pray, and beseech? Not in wonder and need, as I was calling out, but in agony and pain and despair! And did not God abandon them? Did He not turn away from their prayers and beseechings and pains? So it seemed to them, no doubt. So it seemed, until they died. But I saw them, the dead ones, the Six Million who died. They came to me, did they not? They came to me and spoke and demanded and beseeched. And I responded, did I not? Even when the Lord did not? I responded, I was human, and answered, when the Lord did not!

But did He not? Was His silence not an answer? Was His waiting not an answer? Did He not respond with the rise of the Ghetto? Did He not respond with the rise of Israel? Yes? No? Do you say that the Ghetto arose, not God? Do you say that Israel arose and responded and fought, not God? Are you saying that Man responded, not God? Yes?

Well, I agree. For man responded, and that is God's need and His response. Now that I have seen the Six Million and have responded, now I see that that which has responded in me has been God! From God to God. Now that I have responded, I see that the Six Million are satisfied with me. I see that they have seen the Face of God that I have not. I have seen it from afar, indirect. But this is what they desired of me, the Six Million. They have desired that I tell them of my experience of the Faces of God, not of theirs. They no longer hound me, they no longer beseech me. Whatever I tell them, I must tell them out of my own experience; that is what they demand. For it is from there that they speak. We each have seen the face of God, of God becoming!

And you, dear brothers and sisters, you must speak of the names and laws and letters of God! You must speak out of your experience, for that is God speaking in you. You must let us all know what you have seen, for that is what they want, the Six Million. And that is what God wants. How do I know this? He has told me so! And what, pray tell, has He told you? Perhaps He has told you to listen to me further. Perhaps He has told you to hear my tale. For my tale may be similar to yours. If so, then listen, for the

Lord has told me to tell what I see of the Faces of God. He has asked me to tell of His Faces in the ten mystical crowns of the Sephiroth, the ten crowns of the one King, the ten Faces of God which are One Face. He has asked me to tell them in the frame of Kabbalah, in the frame of the continuing and ancient vision of the Jew, but of the Jew enlightened by the thousands of years of experience and reflection. For what has happened since the birth of God's son? Kabbalah has happened. Enlightenment has happened. But also Auschwitz has happened. But the ten Names can carry Auschwitz. And the ten crowns can answer the Trinity. They are one answer. For your answer must count, too. So hear, oh friends! So hear, oh Jew! So hear, oh Gentile! Hear what I have seen of the Face of God! I know that my vision is only one vision; it is incomplete without yours. For your face is also the Face of God.

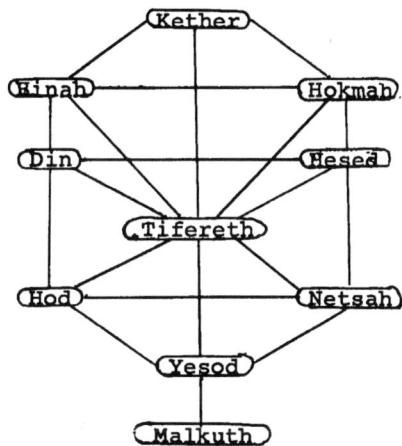

In the beginning is KETHER, the Crown. It is the Supreme Crown, just barely manifest to man, and the link with the Ain Sof, the hidden God, who is always beyond our grasp. Oh Lord, I thank thee for coming into Being in Kether; I thank thee for being King, but I thank thee, too, for always being beyond. I thank thee for never being totally manifest, for as great as Being, as great as the living, as great as the fantastic, marvelous idea of God becoming totally man, there must be a Becoming, there must be a future, a more. For I have seen the face of my own greediness for more, and that, too, must reflect the Face of the God of the beyond, of that which leads me further. And that is the place beyond the Crown. But Crown, too, I must have. KETHER is the beginning, the most mysterious and recondite, which begins with "In."

Can you, dearly beloved, see that Crown? Can you see its jewel-bedecked quality? Can you see the ten tines? see them as pointing up and reaching toward the limitless wonder of the hidden Ain Sof? I see them as pointing down, with the ten faces of the Almighty shared therein, going around the center of Nothingness, and sharing in the One. I see it as the Tree growing upside down from Heaven, the Tree of Kabbalah and of Life, which is eternal; and I see it as the Tree growing from deep in the world, in the earth of Man, and reaching up toward the ever-coming-closer and ever-retreating Ain Sof, the Tree of Knowledge. So, see the Crown, and pray to the two Trees in One.

But come with me, down the grades from the Tree of Heaven, or up from the Tree of Earth, for, as the Crown points, it is pointing up or down. Come with me, as I say, and see the face of HOKMAH, the Wisdom and primordial idea of God. For that First point is the "beginning," as we have said, when God, the Father, moves out of his reconditeness into creation.

Oh point, oh Father, oh wisdom of maleness, of the archetypal idea which moves from the eternal into the temporal, which allows itself to suffer the coming into being! It is a suffering, this becoming, but a joy and a wonder and a greatness. This is the wisdom of the Lord.

And move from the Father, across to the Mother, the BINAH of Understanding and intelligence. For the point of the eternal must be understood and received, must it not? Is not Creation the true creation of Heaven and Earth? Is not the Lord both the Creation and the Reception? The Wisdom and the Understanding? The Father and the Mother? So sayeth even the Kabbalists of old. And so say I. So the women will not be excluded, say we! Small, say you, and shame. Small, say I, but true. For now, the Face of God is the face of opposition, of conflict. Even here. For the One has become two. And the two must flow up and be resolved in the One of KETHER, or flow down and find the lower union, the earthly union, the farther union, all the way down to RAHAMIM or TIFERETH, Compassion and Beauty. This do I know, Oh Lord, this, too, have I experienced. But before, Oh Lord, before You sink and fall so far, let me speak of Your face of HESED, of love and mercy, and of GEVURAH-DIN, of power and stern judgment. I must speak of these, for now Your faces come closer and we, mankind, can taste You and see You and fear You and feel You.

HESED. A male face. One of mercy and kindness, of forgiveness. The Christians, they saw that face as one of the Woman, of Mary. And they, too, were right. For one face can be malely kind and femalely kind. But this kindness, this mercy, is that of the One Lord of Passion who has become peaceful and merciful. The One who can even forgive the Evil One. He can, in short, having discovered His own total opposition with Himself, forgive Himself. HESED. A male face. One of love and mercy.

GEVURAH and DIN. A female face. A face of power. The face, dearly beloved, of Nature Herself. The power of it all: the winds, the rains, the earthquakes. God's face. Female. The power of judgment and passion. And, it is a secret—it is Female. For it needs the power of the Male, of HESED, to restrain it. It needs the mercy of the male to soften it, else too hard, too powerful. And HESED? Without Gevurah, He is nothing. Without the passion and the power, His love is hollow and His mercy insipid. That is not our God, Oh Children of Israel! That is not our God! But beware, Oh Children of Israel, when Male and Female are separated! Beware! For then there is only power and passion and stern judgment—and there is destruction. Or there are only words and rules and regulations and emptiness—and there is destruction.

The two do battle, and they go up, the Male and Female, to the Mother and Father, and up to the Crown. But also they go down; they go down, go the Brother and Sister of Hesed and Gevurah; they go down and unite in RAHAMIM, the compassion of God. They unite in the RAHAMIM of God, who mediates his own Brother-Sister pair, and reconciles His-Her Self in Compassion. He reconciles in compassion, dearly beloved, where power and kindness are One. But, dearly beloved, He reconciles, too, in TIFERETH, in Beauty. For some, Compassion is all they long for of the Lord. But for us, for you and me, who live to create, to adore and to love, we need TIFERETH, the Beauty of God, to sustain us! Oh, TIFERETH, You are the beauty of the Universe before which I weep and am dazzled. Oh, Central Column, all poets know that you are at the Center, for without Beauty, there is no Truth. And, without Truth, Beauty has no existence.

Is there more? The Six Faces of God are enough, are they not? Is not Six the number of Creation? Is not the Creation of Beauty in truth and wisdom enough? What more could the Lord want? What more could we want?

More faces. The Lord goes on, both higher and lower. For there are new opposites, are there not? Out of the grandeur of Beauty, we rise and fall to NETSAH and HOD. NETSAH, victory and lasting endurance. A maleness. And HOD, God's majesty, a femaleness. Are not these opposites, too? Have we not felt the maleness of enduring forever, of staying with the conflict of opposites, of enduring the battles and the wars and the absence of an answer from God? Is this not a maleness? Yes...and no. For now, the victory and endurance and battle are both more abstract and more concrete. When we adore, when we love and bask in the Glory of God, His-Her majesty of HOD, is that Male? Or Female? Yes.

But, more than both, more than the conflict of NETSAH and HOD, of enduring battle and the power of holding on the one side, and the adoration and surrender on the other—more, as I say, than these in God, are the wonder and intense pleasure of their resolution, in YESOD. What is YESOD? YESOD, the "foundation," the basis of all the active forces in God: all the forces of God have descended from the first through the eighth face, and now are united in the ninth, the basis and foundation. Do you know who this is? This is none other than the *Zaddik*, the righteous one, who is the Foundation of the World. For Noah was one, and Moses was one. And David and Solomon. There have been many and many a *Zaddik*. Many and many. And there will be many and many a more. For now, dearly beloved, even Sophie-Sarah will be a *Zaddik*! And how do I know? The Lord has told me so! And you, too, dear friend, you, too, will be a *Zaddik*, for the Lord wants it. He wants us all to be the foundation, the righteous one, the basis of His forces and faces. For your face is the Face of God. Have I not told you? Yes. And you must listen. For then, too, I will listen to you. YESOD, foundation, Zaddik, righteous one: where God becomes human, and incarnates Himself in the world. The ninth place, the place of the Enlightened one, the Righteous of God. And know, all, that this, too, is a He-She place, for all!

And yet, and yet more. Is there still more? Yes, dearly beloved, there is more. There is the tenth. What is the tenth? It is MALKUTH, the Kingdom of God itself. For what is the King, in His totality, in His eight faces, or even in His nine faces which show in the One, or in the One person, if He does not have a community, a Kingship? What is it, this lack of community? It is a narrowness and a lovelessness. And what has the Kingdom, the community, included heretofore? Why, the *Keneseth Israel*, of course. The Chosen People. The community of the Chosen. And this, dear brothers and sisters, will continue. But the Lord has told me that His Community is the World. The Lord has told me, even, that there are Worlds beyond Worlds, but that His incarnation in us all, will lead to the KINGDOM OF GOD UPON EARTH. The world will be made up of Zaddikim, dearly beloved, of male and female Zaddikim! It will be a world of the Heavenly Jerusalem come to Earth. And that is the *Shekhinah*: when the Lord will be totally united with His Kingdom, in us as individuals and as a world. It is coming, dearly beloved. It is coming. The King will have His crown, facing up and down. The King will have his Kingship, facing up and down.

And this is the work of us all: to become *Zaddikim* in the service of the Lord, and the coming of His Kingship. It has happened, it is happening, it will happen. Thus is the Tree of the Lord! And thus is the picture of humankind, of Adam Kadmon, the primordial man/woman and the future man/woman. For we are all he, are we not?

And that is why I am here, my nine friends. For I knew it when I spoke of the faces. I knew that I would be both myself as a *Zaddik* and included in a *Minyan* of ten. And I know that we ten are symbolic of the Minyan of the World. I know that this tree we look at together, the Tree of Life and the Tree of Knowledge, is One. All humankind will see it one day, whether it takes two incarnations or hundreds! We know it, we ten. My friends, my brothers and sisters, I embrace you. We know it. That is our message.

Let us tell it to the world.